# Praise for *You and Your Adult Child*

"Provides clear guidelines for avoiding arguments and creating more effective bonds."

—Jancee Dunn, *The New York Times*

"If you're the parent of a young adult, you need this book. Larry Steinberg—one of my favorite thinkers and writers—offers clear, cogent answers to all the questions you're wrestling with right now. Basically, this book is the next best thing to having this world-renowned psychologist on speed-dial."

—Angela Duckworth, Ph.D., author of
*Grit: The Power of Passion and Perseverance*

"Steinberg distills decades of wisdom and experience into the sensitive, straight-shooting guide that parents of grown children have been waiting for. With deep compassion for all involved, *You and Your Adult Child* details exactly when, why, and how to address the toughest topics—from mental health to finances to sex. I will be recommending this practical, research-backed, clear-eyed book to every parent I know."

—Lisa Damour, Ph.D., author of *Untangled*
and *The Emotional Lives of Teenagers*

"This compassionate, practical guide applies the wisdom of a leading expert on human development to our relationships with adult children. Filled with stories and science, this book will benefit grandparent, parent, and child alike—a gift that will keep on giving across the generations."

—Daniel J. Siegel, M.D., *New York Times* bestselling author of
*IntraConnected*, *Mindsight*, and *Brainstorm*.

"A highly useful, wonderfully innovative guide to parenting adult children. I can think of no finer shepherd to take us through this difficult and underexplored terrain. Whether he's reframing our expectations or explaining how to give delicate advice to skittish twentysomethings, Steinberg writes with insight and empathy."

—Jennifer Senior, winner of the 2022 Pulitzer Prize for Feature Writing and author of the *New York Times* bestseller *All Joy and No Fun*

"There is more wisdom and more good sense here than in any book I have ever read about parenting. And it is science-based to boot. A must-read for parents of adult children."

—Martin Seligman, Ph.D., author of *The Hope Circuit* and coauthor of *Tomorrowmind*

"In my forty-plus years of being a parent and a psychologist, Steinberg has been my go-to every step of the way. With his usual mix of science, clinical experience, and thoughtful practicality, he helps us temper our expectations and understand how young adults can best adjust to a rapidly changing world. If you have grown children, whether they are flourishing or floundering, *You and Your Adult Child* is essential reading."

—Madeline Levine, Ph.D., author of *The Price of Privilege*, *Teach Your Children Well*, and *Ready or Not*

"Steinberg combines decades of experience as a professor, developmental psychologist, and father with the most up-to-date research in the field to offer the guide all parents of adult children need. This thoughtful, inspiring book is a clear blueprint for how our role as parents can successfully evolve as we offer our kids support and encouragement in their newly independent lives."

—Lisa Heffernan, *New York Times* bestselling author and cofounder of *Grown & Flown* website

"Steinberg is a world-class expert in the science of human development, but what matters most in this helpful book is his voice—that of a wise, empathetic friend who has studied how to maintain the precious parent-child bond far into the child's adulthood and wants to share what he knows."

—Robin Marantz Henig, coauthor (with Samantha Henig) of *Twentysomething: Why Do Young Adults Seem Stuck?*

"I'm deeply grateful for this empowering, invaluable guide as my own children pass from adolescence into the rapidly changing terrain of modern adulthood."

—Jessica Lahey, *New York Times* bestselling
author of *The Gift of Failure*

"*You and Your Adult Child* is a treasure for today's parents and their adult children! Steinberg helps us take a fresh look at the multiple changes in norms, timetables, expectations, and opportunities for the current generation of young adults. No wonder we often see things through different lenses! An engaging writer with empathy for both generations, he provides practical principles and techniques for solving conflicts and enhancing relationships."

—Karen Levin Coburn, coauthor of *Letting Go:
A Parents' Guide to Understanding the College Years*

"Here at last is a no-shame, no-blame guide for moms and dads of grown-up 'kids' in their twenties and thirties. With his signature mix of expertise and empathy, Steinberg offers sage guidance for how to parent without overparenting, how to speak to be heard, and how to set boundaries while maintaining, even deepening, loving bonds. It's the kind of book you'll come back to over and over for years to come."

—Judith Warner, author of *And Then They Stopped Talking to Me:
Making Sense of Middle School* and *Perfect Madness:
Motherhood in the Age of Anxiety*

"When our kids reach young adulthood, we parents face a host of fresh questions. Do you want to know when you should give your opinion or bite your tongue? Are you anxious about their college choices? Worried about their mental health? Miss them terribly when they're away but want to evict them an hour after they get home? If you can relate to any of these situations, *You and Your Adult Child* is a must-read, filled with thoughtful, informed, and compassionate advice."

—Rosalind Wiseman, *New York Times* bestselling author of
*Queen Bees and Wannabes*

"During this century, the challenges facing young adults have increased dramatically, as has research on how to address these challenges. Steinberg combines the latest findings with timeless wisdom to offer parents of people in their 20s and 30s a uniquely empowering, invaluable guide to helping their kids make the most of these decades."

—Carol Dweck, Ph.D., professor of psychology
at Stanford University and author of
*Mindset: The New Psychology of Success*

"Parenting never ends, but until now, parents of grown children lacked a comprehensive guide to this period. Thankfully, the wait is finally over. Steinberg's practical, myth-shattering, inspiring book shows how we and our adult kids can thrive together."

—Michele Borba, Ed.D., educational psychologist
and author of *Thrivers*

## Books by Laurence Steinberg

*You and Your Adolescent: The Essential Guide for Ages 10–25*

*The Ten Basic Principles of Good Parenting*

*Age of Opportunity: Lessons from the New Science of Adolescence*

*Crossing Paths: How Your Child's Adolescence Triggers Your Own Crisis*
(with Wendy Steinberg)

*Beyond the Classroom: Why School Reform Has Failed and What Parents
Need to Do* (with B. Bradford Brown and Sanford M. Dornbusch)

*Rethinking Juvenile Justice* (with Elizabeth S. Scott)

*When Teenagers Work: The Psychological and Social Costs of
Adolescent Employment* (with Ellen Greenberger)

# YOU AND YOUR ADULT CHILD

## How to Grow Together in Challenging Times

Laurence Steinberg, Ph.D.

SIMON & SCHUSTER PAPERBACKS

NEW YORK   LONDON   TORONTO   SYDNEY   NEW DELHI

An Imprint of Simon & Schuster, LLC
1230 Avenue of the Americas
New York, NY 10020

First Simon & Schuster trade paperback edition March 2024

SIMON & SCHUSTER PAPERBACKS and colophon are registered trademarks of Simon & Schuster, LLC

Simon & Schuster: Celebrating 100 Years of Publishing in 2024

For information about special discounts for bulk purchases, please contact Simon & Schuster Special Sales at 1-866-506-1949 or business@simonandschuster.com.

The Simon & Schuster Speakers Bureau can bring authors to your live event. For more information or to book an event, contact the Simon & Schuster Speakers Bureau at 1-866-248-3049 or visit our website at www.simonspeakers.com.

*Interior design by Alexis Minieri*

Manufactured in the United States of America

1   3   5   7   9   10   8   6   4   2

Library of Congress Cataloging-in-Publication Data has been applied for.

ISBN 978-1-6680-0948-2
ISBN 978-1-6680-0949-9 (pbk)
ISBN 978-1-6680-0950-5 (ebook)

For Ben and Ashley

# Contents

# CONTENTS

# Introduction

Today about 65 million parents in the United States have one or more children in their twenties and thirties. Like parents at any stage, those with adult children also find they need advice, recommendations, guidance, and reassurance. As children get older, the demands of parenting change, but the challenges never disappear. No matter how well our children are doing or how much they're struggling, parenting never ends, nor do the uncertainties it brings. You may have thought that the tough part of parenting was over once your kid was no longer a teenager, but you've discovered that being the parent of an adult child is challenging in its own right. Some parents find this stage even more demanding than adolescence had been.

I'm a psychologist with nearly fifty years of experience researching, teaching, and writing about parenthood and psychological development. I've been speaking to parent groups for decades, usually in schools or communities concerned about raising children and adolescents. I always leave time to respond to audience questions, and I usually hang around after my presentations to chat with parents who were uncomfortable posing their questions in front of the whole audience.

Decades ago, I would mainly field questions about raising teenagers. Although I still get a lot of these inquiries, I've noticed that, more and more, parents worry about how to manage their relationships with their grown children. "How do I know if my son is floundering?" "Is it okay to help my daughter with her grad school application?" "What should I do if my kid is moving in with someone I think is dangerous?" "We have been helping our twenty-five-year-old financially for the last few years, but how long is too long?" "My son has moved back home, and we can't seem to agree on rules for living together. He spends a lot of time on the couch playing video games, but my wife and I think he should be spending his time looking for a job every day."

I'm also a father and a grandfather. I know firsthand that the most important tool a parent can have is an accurate understanding of where their child is developmentally and how this influences their thoughts, behavior, and emotions. Think of the relief you felt when your toddler and, later, teenager pulled away—often angrily—and an expert calmly told you, "That's developmentally appropriate." This knowledge helps you develop reasonable expectations, which are critical to your success as a parent.

Unfortunately, parents of adult children lack the resources that are available for parents of infants, schoolchildren, or teenagers. True, you can find books here and there written by or for despairing parents who are estranged from their grown children. (Hopefully, you aren't estranged from your adult child; I cover this topic in chapter 3.) But you probably have questions about how to deal with the challenges of parenting an adult child. And all of us can benefit from advice on how to navigate or even avoid common minefields. *You and Your Adult Child* is the first comprehensive guide for *all* parents whose children are in their twenties or thirties.

This book is based on my own research as well as groundbreaking work by my colleagues. It also benefits from my more than four decades of teaching undergraduates and graduate students and my thirty-eight years as a parent. From that well of experience, I draw advice for virtually every difficulty you and your adult child might face regarding their mental health, education, finances, romantic relationships, and child-rearing. I illustrate these challenges throughout the book with anecdotes about parents and their adult children; the families are composites based on conversations I've had with many parents, as well as relevant research, but I have changed important details to protect the families' anonymity.

When I began writing this book, I quickly realized we don't have a simple, common term to describe children in their twenties or thirties, the way we have labels like "infants," "toddlers," or "teenagers." That's probably because, until recently, discussions of this age group focused on them as students, employees, or spouses, but not as people who have ongoing bonds with their parents. Try as I might, I couldn't come up with a term that wasn't cumbersome or derogatory. So, for lack of a better blanket term, I use "adult children" and "grown children" interchangeably to describe offspring of a certain age, not people of questionable emotional maturity.

The book begins with some general principles that inform later chapters on specific issues, like handling finances, your child's romantic partner, or concerns about your child's parenting. In chapter 1, I discuss how parenting an adult child is different today than it was a generation ago, how your role as a parent has changed now that your child is an adult, and how to balance your natural desire to remain involved in your child's life with their need to establish some autonomy from you. Chapter 2 discusses how to maintain a healthy day-to-day relationship with your child, including deciding whether to speak up or bite your tongue when you have concerns, understanding and managing the complicated emotions that having an adult child often trigger, resolving conflicts with your child constructively, and handling disagreements with your partner over how to parent. Chapter 3 provides advice on how to take care of your child's and your own mental health and the causes of estrangement between adult children and their parents.

Following these introductory chapters, I turn to specific challenges that often arise in connection with your child's education, finances, and romantic relationships. In each chapter, I explore the issues that usually arise at different phases of your relationship with your kid. Chapter 4 provides advice on matters that frequently surface when your adult child is a student, like how much you should be involved in their college education, alternatives to traditional college, and handling visits home from school. Chapter 5 addresses questions you may have about providing financial support to your child once they've finished school, helping them buy a home, and discussing your own personal finances with them. Chapter 6 looks at a variety of issues concerning your child's romantic life, including revelations about their sexuality, their choice of a partner, maintaining good relations with your child and their partner, and helping a child weather marital difficulties or divorce.

These discussions set the stage for chapter 7, which addresses the most frequent question I'm asked by parents with adult children: Is my child floundering—struggling to get their footing—and, if so, what can I do to help? (I also describe adult children who are flourishing—doing exceptionally well.) I focus on four common sources of parental concern about their kid's progress and suggest ways to judge how things are going in the realms of work, school, romance, and residence: taking a long time to finish school, problems finding and settling into a career, having difficulty establishing a committed relationship, and moving back into their parents' home. In each instance, I suggest ways parents can respond to help kids who appear to be floundering.

Chapter 8 looks at your role as a grandparent, including how best to help an adult child who is a new parent, whether to voice concerns or give advice about your child's parenting, and how to develop a strong bond with your grandchild. I conclude with chapter 9, which summarizes the key points of the book, lists steps that parents can take to strengthen their relationship with their adult child, and looks ahead to how your relationship with your child will continue to change as they enter their forties.

I had many audiences in mind while writing this book: Parents who are approaching this stage of parenthood and want to know what to expect. Parents who are already in the thick of it, think things are going well, but believe there's room for improvement. And parents who are having a tough time, or feel lost and confused, maybe even desperate, and want advice on what to do. Regardless of which of these three categories best describes you, I hope this book will help you to be a more relaxed, more informed, more capable, more confident parent.

One of the book's major themes concerns the many ways young adulthood has changed since we were that age. You're probably aware of this in the abstract—it would be hard not to be, given how much has been said in the media about millennials (people born during the 1980s and the first half of the 1990s) and Generation Z (born in the second half of the 1990s or later, and sometimes referred to as "postmillennials"). But little has been said about what the social and economic changes of the past forty years mean for you as a parent or how to best adapt your expectations, attitudes, and behavior to today's realities.

So, let's start by looking at how much times have changed, and why being a young adult today is so different than it was when we were their age.

## CHAPTER ONE

# Your Evolving Role as a Parent

## Times Have Changed

Today, we need a guide to parenting adult children more than ever before, for several reasons: parents have changed, young people have changed, our scientific understanding of young adulthood has changed, and times have changed. So many of us assumed that we'd be done with parenting by the time our kids finished college, moved away from home, or got married. But parenting today is not what it was when we grew up, and neither is young adulthood. And that might be perplexing, even frustrating.

❧

*How parents have changed.* When I was about thirty years old, I went through a very rough patch with my parents. My wife and I were planning our wedding, and I thought my parents were being difficult and stubborn in their disapproval of certain decisions we had made about the ceremony and the reception. (Differences between parents and adult children about wedding arrangements are common, as I'll discuss in chapter 6.) To her credit, my wife tried her best to mediate between us, but neither I nor my parents would budge, and we remained on bad terms throughout the planning and during the wedding itself.

At the wedding, my parents made no attempt to hide their displeasure. I was so angry at them for spoiling the mood that I didn't call them before my wife and I left for our honeymoon the next day. It wasn't until our son was born, about two years later, that our rift began to heal. Ensuring that our son had a good relationship with his grandparents was more important to all of us than holding on to the grudge.

After my parents and I reconciled, I wanted to talk to my dad about what had happened between us. I fought frequently with my mother during my teens, so being on the outs with her wasn't new for me. But this dispute was the first time I'd undergone anything more than a brief disagreement with my father, with whom I'd always been close.

One night, after dinner at my parents' house, he and I stayed up and had a nightcap. Once we'd run through our usual topics—politics, our jobs, sports, etc.—I paused and said I wanted to talk about our relationship.

He looked at me as if I wanted to discuss time travel or space aliens. "What relationship? I'm your father."

It's hard to imagine a parent saying something like that to their child now. But my father, born in the 1920s, was very much a man of his generation. He had served in the military; he was stoical and unemotional—although he was also kind, caring, and attentive. It just wasn't his style to talk about feelings or relationships.

Today's parents of adult children grew up in a completely different cultural climate, in which talking about and analyzing relationships is commonplace, even expected, and parents define their roles very differently than my father and his peers did. I can't imagine my parents reading a book on child-rearing, except perhaps Dr. Spock's *Baby and Child Care*, and even then only to look up something concrete, like when to start solid food or how to ease the pain of teething.

In contrast, today's parents of young adults have a long history of continual hands-on involvement in their children's lives, from researching preschools to overseeing—or even helping to write—college applications. Parents may wonder whether there's any reason to change course just because their child is now an adult.

These parents also stay in close touch with their kids. Many college students and recent graduates communicate with their parents several times a day, talking, texting, and sharing posts on social media. Some of my students have told me that when they're in the midst of midterms and finals, they have to turn their devices off so they can block distracting messages from their parents.

In many respects, this frequent contact is great. Many young people and their parents are closer and more knowledgeable about each other's lives than ever before. But this intimacy has eroded some important generational boundaries and inadvertently granted adult children permission to treat their parents more like equals than they had in the past, which may have created strain in their relationship, especially when parents assumed that their kids would defer to them when they disagreed.

The increased intimacy also allows parents to learn about aspects of their children's lives that may lead them to worry more about their kids' physical and emotional health and how they and their kids are getting along. (True, twentieth-century parents were known to say, "Why don't you call?" but usually if their children had been out of touch for a week or two, not for a couple of days.) Nowadays, if parents with grown children sense there's a problem in their relationship, they want to know then and there what they can do to make things right. So, in every way possible, today's parents are much more deeply enmeshed in the lives of their adult children than previous generations of parents were.

⁂

*How young people have changed.* The biggest transformation among young people is that they now take longer to move fully into the conventional roles of adulthood. It takes them longer to finish their education, become financially independent, settle into marriage (or a comparable arrangement), establish their own residence, and have kids of their own.

As just one example of the impact of these longer time frames, consider how settling into a romantic relationship has changed in the last few decades. Parents have always been concerned about their children's choice of partners, but in the past, any worries they had would arise mainly during the high school or college years. Given how young and inexperienced their kids were with romance at this age, it was natural for parents to speak up if they thought their child was getting involved with someone problematic. Today, parents often watch from the sidelines as their grown children go through a series of serious relationships during their twenties and well into their thirties—a process that has probably been prolonged by online dating, which makes false starts more likely.

There's no question that the transition into adulthood is later and longer today than ever before. The language used to describe the lengthened transition is revealing, though. Some pundits have wondered why it's "taking so long for people to grow up," implying that anyone who isn't hitting various milestones on some arbitrary schedule is immature or even just plain lazy. Others lament how many people are "prolonging adolescence," which to my ear sounds like accusing kids of being self-indulgent or overly anxious. Still others describe what they see as a "failure to launch," some sort of deficiency or incompetence.

This view derives from the premise that healthy development is furthered by the demands of adulthood—the responsibilities of marriage and parenting, the requirements of a job, the challenges of self-sufficiency. By implication, someone who hasn't accomplished these milestones on time must be immature.

This view is wrong. There's no scientific evidence that delaying the entrance into adulthood has stunted young people's psychological development. This is a really important fact that parents often have a hard time understanding. Moreover, as I'll explain next, new research about adolescent brain development suggests that, under the right conditions, delaying adulthood actually enhances the brain's development by keeping it malleable for a longer period of time.

⁂

*Science has changed our understanding of young adulthood.* Even if you don't read any other section of this book closely, do read this—I've found it can drastically change how we parents look at our kids. Historically, developmental psychologists have more or less ignored both young adulthood and, except for an unwarranted fascination with the "midlife crisis," middle adulthood as well. They just assumed that people stopped maturing at the end of adolescence—say around age eighteen—and experienced no further change in psychological functioning until a decline in old age. Experts assumed that people between twenty and sixty-five are affected by specific life experiences, like getting married or divorced, promoted or laid off, but unlike other stages of life, young and middle-aged adults didn't change in predictable ways, as infants, children, adolescents, and the elderly do.

This assumption is only partly correct. New research shows this isn't the case for the period between twenty and twenty-five. During these five years, substantial changes take place in the brain's anatomy and activity that have an enormous impact on how young adults function and tremendous implications for parents' understanding of their adult children.

Developmental neuroscientists—experts who study how the brain's anatomy and activity change with age—have only recently turned their attention to brain development after age eighteen. They've made two discoveries that are changing the way we view young people—and should change the way you look at your kids.

The first revelation is that the brain is still very responsive to the environment during the young adult years—what scientists call "plasticity"—the extent to which experience can change the brain. We've long known that it's very malleable during the early years. This is why psychologists, public health experts, and educators have been so concerned about providing adequate childcare and education for young kids, whose brains are primed to take advantage of rich, nurturing experiences.

But the last two decades have seen a growing recognition that another burst of plasticity takes place at the beginning of adolescence and may continue into the mid-twenties—as long as people receive adequate environmental stimulation, which is necessary to keep the brain malleable for a longer time.

For reasons we don't yet understand, this window of heightened plasticity begins to close as people enter adulthood, around age twenty-five. This means that the impact of delaying the transition into adulthood depends on how these years are spent. Under the right conditions—which include exposing people to challenge and novelty—staying in adolescence a little longer may lengthen the amount of time that the brain can profit most from stimulation.

Unfortunately, plasticity is a double-edged sword. When the brain is highly responsive to the environment, it's sensitive to both good and bad experiences. Good experiences provide opportunities for continued learning and cognitive development. Toxic ones, though, are more harmful to the adolescent brain than they are after the mid-twenties. As we'll see in chapter 3, this is why adolescence and young adulthood are times of heightened vulnerability to stress, trauma, deprivation, and addictive substances.

A second important discovery about the period from twenty to twenty-five is the sheer extent of brain maturation during these years, especially in regions that govern self-control. Young adults are more mature than teenagers, but they're still not as mature as people in their late twenties. They're still developing the capacity to rein in their impulses, emotions, and susceptibility to peers, which explains why so many risky behaviors—like crime, binge drinking, reckless driving, and unsafe sex—peak during this stage, and why so much of this risky behavior occurs in groups. You may still need to have discussions from time to time to raise concerns you have about a risky or reckless decision your child has made. Don't be surprised if this is the case.

❧

*How society has changed.* Delays in one aspect of the transition into adulthood often provoke changes in another realm. Consider alterations in the nature of work. Today's jobs require more years of schooling than they did a generation ago (whether they genuinely need to is a different matter). This development leads more young people to stay in school longer, either to pursue education beyond college or to pick up additional skills as undergraduates. In fact, what we quaintly refer to as a "four-year degree" now takes the average U.S. college student five years or more.

The lengthening of education has had cascading effects on other parts of young adults' lives. More years of school delays entry into a full-time, career-related occupation, which often prolongs economic dependence on parents. As a consequence of these changes, getting married and setting up an independent household are also delayed, which often pushes parenthood well into the future.

It's hard to quantify just how much longer it takes to become an adult now than it did in the past because the transition isn't defined by a single event. Let's say we mark the beginning of this process with graduation from college and mark the end with starting a family. True, not everyone does each of these, but it's a useful means of constructing a timeline to show how the length of the transition has changed across generations. The majority of middle-class Americans finish college, most of them marry, and most become parents, usually in that order. This is true today, just as it was a generation ago.

According to my calculations, using statistics published by the Census Bureau and other government agencies, today it takes the average middle-class young adult about thirteen years to go from graduation to starting a family. It took their parents' generation about eight years to make the same journey.

A five-year difference may not seem like much, but it should alter the metric by which you evaluate your child's progress. Someone who hasn't yet settled down by the age of thirty may seem like a slacker to their parents, but they may be right on schedule by today's standards.

We parents need to adjust to this new timetable. Delays in entering adult roles will probably become more widespread because the educational requirements of good jobs are increasing, not declining. The longer people stay in school, the more likely they are to delay full-time employment, financial independence, marriage, and parenthood.

Complicating matters is parents' tendency to compare their grown child's "progress" against the timetable that they, the parents, followed when they were growing up. And, if you have more than one child, it can be difficult to judge each one's journey through adulthood compared to their sibling's, because even if they grew up in the same household, they may have different personalities, talents, and ambitions.

It's hard for today's parents to view unmarried, financially dependent thirtysomethings who haven't yet settled into a career or stable relationship without worrying that their child, or they, might have done something wrong. Not surprisingly, many parents wonder if their child is floundering or doing fine. In chapter 7, I'll explain how to tell the difference.

These widespread changes in the normal timetable of adulthood have been exacerbated by the monumental societal changes of recent years. Events like the Great Recession of 2008 and the COVID-19 pandemic created considerable financial and logistical stresses for people in their twenties and thirties. With higher housing costs, many kids have had to move back to their parents' home or ask for financial assistance. Parents have been forced to become even more involved in their adult children's lives than they ever anticipated, or perhaps desired.

All these changes—in kids, parents, scientific understanding, and society—require parents to think differently about what their role is as the parent of an adult.

## Your Role Has Changed

In many ways, the main elements of successfully parenting an adult child are similar to those in previous stages: be generous in expressing love and support, be involved in your child's life without being intrusive, listen to their point of view, treat them with respect, and be there when they need you.

But it's also important to understand how your role as a parent has changed. During infancy and early childhood, you provided care, nourishment, stimulation, and security. During the elementary school years, you continued to do these things, but you also provided structure and organization to help your child do well in school, make friends, feel competent and confident, and develop empathy and ethics. During adolescence, your role shifted toward providing guidance and advice rather than active management, and helping your teenager develop responsibility, autonomy, and the beginnings of a moral compass.

If you were successful in these early stages, you'll have contributed to raising a confident, compassionate, successful, and ethical young person who has a reasonably clear understanding of themselves, the basic skills necessary to function independently in the world, a satisfying network of close friendships and family bonds, and the capacity to form a strong relationship with a romantic partner.

Now that you've helped your child reach most or all of these milestones, your role is to help turn their skills and capacities into realities. As I'll explain, this requires being supportive and involved, but in a way that doesn't squelch your child's sense of autonomy.

To do this well, though, you'll need to approach your role as a parent with different expectations than those you brought to your child's younger years.

## Adjusting Your Expectations

When she was a teenager, Gina spent every Easter at home with her parents and two younger sisters. In March of her junior year at college, Gina phoned home to say she was planning to accept an invitation to spend the upcoming holiday at her roommate's house. She explained to her mother that during their fall semester abroad, she'd had a chance to get to know her roommate's family well when they visited their daughter in Florence for a week. She casually said she thought it would be fun to do something different this year—after spending the past twenty Easters doing the same thing with the family. Her mother was disappointed, and said as much, which led to a heated conversation that ended angrily with her hanging up on her daughter.

After several weeks had passed and Gina and her mother got some distance on the matter, they agreed that Gina would usually spend Easter at home but for occasional exceptions, as long as she lets her parents know well in advance. Down the road, if Gina marries, her mother may need to do another recalibration about Easter gatherings depending on what Gina and her spouse work out between themselves.

While parents' expectations may be unrealistic, they're usually understandable. Often, however, they hold on to beliefs that are no longer appropriate. What made sense five years ago, when your child was still living at home, may no longer be feasible now that they're living on their own.

When your kid was in college, you probably got a daily call or text from them. Expecting this from a twenty-four-year-old who's now managing a full-time job and living on their own may strike them as out of line.

If you called your parents several times a week when you were in your late twenties, you may think that expecting a call every Sunday afternoon from your twenty-eight-year-old is perfectly reasonable. But if your child's partner speaks to their parents just twice a month, and not always at the same time, your expectation may strike your child as intrusive, maybe even embarrassing, for them to fulfill.

There isn't a right or wrong answer about how often parents and their adult children should be in touch, of course. But understanding that you and your child may be coming at this issue from different perspectives may stop you from concluding that something is amiss just because they don't call as often as you like.

❧

Ask yourself what you expect from your relationship with your adult child. It's especially important to find out whether you and your partner have similar expectations so that your child isn't getting mixed messages from their parents. You and your partner may have been on the same page when your child was a teenager, but it's possible, even likely, that each of you has since developed your own ideas about how to parent, and those views may not align perfectly.

Howard and his ex-wife, Samantha, disagreed about whether they would subsidize their daughter's income now that she had finished school and moved to Los Angeles to become a screenwriter. Alissa was living off her salary as a waitress while writing after her restaurant shift, well into the early morning hours. Because her take-home pay wasn't enough to rent her own place, she had to share a one-bedroom apartment with two other women, whose friends often stopped by at night and whose voices were easily heard through the thin wall that separated the living room and bedroom.

After a few months, Alissa asked her parents if they could help her rent a small studio apartment, where she'd have more space and quiet time to write. Her parents had different reactions to this proposal. Her father had assumed that once Alissa had finished school, she would no longer depend on her parents to support her. Her mother believed they should supplement Alissa's income until she sold her first script.

After they talked it over, they decided they would help her out for one year and then reassess the situation. When they had disagreed about such things in the past—like how much spending money they would give Alissa in college—Howard and Samantha had often split the difference. It was an effective way of keeping their divorce amicable, and it kept Alissa from playing them off against each other. Presenting a united front made their lives easier, and it made Alissa's life easier, too, since she was more likely to accept without complaint the decision her parents had made together.

※

Harboring unreasonably high expectations of your adult child will only lead to conflict, but so will deliberately low expectations.

We don't ordinarily see them as such, but neuroscientists think of expectations as predictions. When you wake up on your birthday expecting that your kid will call later that morning, you're making a prediction that this will happen.

Whether our predictions about an event are confirmed or contradicted has a profound impact on how we view and feel about what actually occurs, separate from whether the outcome itself is desirable or undesirable. This is because the part of our brain that creates and monitors our expectations works independently from the part that decides whether events are rewarding or disappointing, and the brain's expectation region values *accuracy* above all else. Our ultimate feeling about an event is a mixture of how it turned out and how accurate our expectations were.

When we have a bad experience, we're disappointed, but not quite as much if this is what we'd expected. By the same token, when we expect a bad experience but actually have a good one, we don't feel quite as happy as we would if we'd accurately predicted the experience would be positive. An accurate expectation adds to the enjoyment of a positive experience and diminishes the disappointment of a negative one. If your child invites you to dinner and you have a good time, you'll enjoy it more if you'd gone in with positive expectations than if you'd been nervous about how the evening would go. Being pleasantly surprised feels good, of course, but not as good as having positive expectations confirmed.

So, it doesn't make sense to have unreasonably high *or* unreasonably low expectations.

❧

Parents often need to revise their expectations about how much their adult child will tell them about milestones in their life. This can be especially disappointing to parents who expect that, now that their child is an adult, they'll have much more to share with each other, like the ups and downs of work, marriage, or parenthood. But it's quite possible—and quite normal—that our children will reveal less about themselves than they used to.

It's often true that your kid doesn't feel comfortable telling you bad news. Maybe they don't want you to know they've been laid off, were dumped by someone, or want to withdraw their toddler from the preschool that required six months' prepaid tuition. These might be topics they'd prefer to discuss first with peers, who are more likely to be dealing with similar challenges. Sometimes after a bad experience, we want empathy more than the comfort or advice we'd expect from a parent.

Your kid might also hesitate to share promising news, like a positive early pregnancy test, or a possible promotion at work, or meeting someone they envision as a future spouse. They may understandably want to wait until the pregnancy is further along, the promotion goes through, or the relationship has lasted a few months.

The other reason for your child's reticence is hard for parents to accept: by and large, our kids don't think about us nearly as much as we think about them.

Young adulthood is a very busy time. It's unlikely your kid will forget to mention that they got engaged, took a new job across the country, or found a new apartment. But it may not even occur to them to tell you they had a successful performance review at work, ran into a close friend from high school, or made plans to rent a beach house with some colleagues—even though you'd love to hear about all of these things.

Not hearing this kind of news is especially tough when you learn your child has already shared it with friends, coworkers, siblings, cousins—maybe even your spouse. It's hard for parents to discover just how low they rank on their child's priority list, at least with respect to sharing news about their life.

Just as they did as teenagers, many young adults put a premium on relationships with their friends. Part of this includes updating each other on the important (or even mundane) vicissitudes of everyday life. Rather than feel hurt because you're the "last to know," try to take pleasure in the fact that your kid has other people they can depend on and confide in. This network doesn't diminish your importance. And you're probably still among the first to know about the things that really matter.

You might also have inaccurate expectations about how much

advice or help (other than financial assistance, which I discuss in chapter 5) you should be giving. Before we go any further, though, I want to distinguish between help they ask for and unsolicited help you offer.

Unless you and your child are totally estranged or live far away from each other, there will likely be times when they seek your help. If you're a handy mechanic, and your child needs help making a minor repair on their car, it's reasonable for you to expect that they might ask for a hand, and just as reasonable for you to offer one. If your child is a parent, it's reasonable to be asked to babysit every once in a while. But it's just as reasonable for your child to not ask for your help when you thought they would— maybe they have a friend who's a great mechanic—and equally reasonable for you to say you're busy and can't watch the baby that afternoon.

It's realistic for you to expect that your child will ask for assistance only when they truly need your help (when they wouldn't be able to accomplish something crucial without you), to not burden you with excessive requests (regularly asking you for things that they can easily take care of without you), and to understand when you can't help for whatever reason. At the same time, it's reasonable for you to offer help when your child asks for it (or hints strongly at it) or to decline when you're not available or up to it. A good way to avoid bad feelings is to be candid with your kid when you feel unfairly burdened, and to ask them to be honest with you if they ever think you ought to be doing more—or less. This will minimize the chances that one of you might think the other is being selfish or inconsiderate.

Whether you should give *unsolicited* assistance or advice is a trickier issue. Most young adults feel a strong and natural need for autonomy, and even your well-meant offers of assistance or advice may clash with this need. You may be surprised to discover how touchy your kid can be in these situations. That's why it's usually best to let them ask rather than offering your help.

## Respecting Your Child's Autonomy

Most disagreements between parents and their grown children stem from the adult child's continuing need to individuate—to insert some emotional distance into the relationship. The issues vary—money, living arrangements, parenting, and so on—but the conflicts often stem from the child's need for autonomy. Understanding the roots of this need, and knowing how to deal with the challenges it often provokes, are fundamental to maintaining a good relationship with your child.

Children individuate to prove to their parents, to others, and, most important, to themselves that they're their own person. As they grow older, children change how they think about themselves, about their parents, and about the parent-child relationship itself. Some of this takes place consciously (although not usually deliberately), but much of it is unconscious. Although individuation seems like a process in which parents are passive targets of their children's changing views, this isn't the case. Parents play an important role in their child's emotional development, whether by accepting these changes or resisting them.

Toddlerhood and adolescence are the two main stages that come to mind when we think about individuation. The three-year-old who always seems to be shouting, "No!" in response to their parents' requests ("Put your coat on before you go outside," "Please pick your toys up off the floor before someone trips on them," or "It's time for your bath," for example) is really saying, "I'm a person with a will of my own."

The teenager who debates their parents about everything from politics and popular culture to a 10:00 p.m. curfew is really saying, "I'm old enough to have opinions of my own."

Something similar, and just as significant, is also going on around age thirty. To gain some perspective on adult children's need to individuate, it's helpful to look back at what was happening during toddlerhood and early adolescence, because there are important parallels between these stages and what occurs around age thirty. There are also lessons to be learned about what you, as the parent of an adult child, do that either helps or hinders the process.

Although the individuation process that young adults go through shares many characteristics with the one that takes place at three or thirteen, there are important differences. The toddler's quest for individuation is about establishing themselves as a separate person, and the adolescent's is about establishing themselves as someone with their own opinions. The young adult wants to manage life independently, without relying on their parents. And, as was the case during previous stages, the point of individuation as a thirtysomething is to send a message to parents, the rest of the world, and, most important, oneself: "I'm mature enough to handle the responsibilities of adulthood without my parents' help."

Knowing this should help you better understand your child's occasional rejection of your opinions, assistance, or support, even when such rebuffs strike you as illogical or insulting.

*You always loved my taste*, you think to yourself when your child bristles as you gently suggest that the palette they've selected for their living room might be a little garish.

"Whenever I told you about how I solved a problem I was having with someone at the office, you used to tell me I was so great at dealing with other people," you say under your breath as your child rolls their eyes at your suggestion for how to handle a difficult coworker—even though you've managed dozens of similar situations in your own career.

"I can't understand why you won't let me help you with this—it would be so much easier for us to put this dresser together than for you to do it alone," you say, only to be glared at.

Of course, all of this could simply mean that your child's opinions about interior design are no longer the same as yours, that they don't think your approach to office politics is relevant in today's workplace, or that they like working alone on household projects.

But there's a good chance something else is going on, perhaps unconsciously. At age thirty, your child still may be somewhat unsure of their taste, social acumen, or carpentry skills, but involving you will exacerbate their feelings of insecurity, not inspire confidence.

❧

Although conflicts over autonomy are common at this time, their intensity varies from one family to the next. One factor that affects the frequency and degree of these disputes is the cultural context. Autonomy is highly valued in Western societies, especially in the United States, where independence from one's parents is seen as a mark of maturity. Although parents and teenagers often disagree about how and how much young people should show their independence, by the time they're adults, wanting more freedom from parents is not only tolerated but expected. Indeed, American parents tend to worry about their adult children when they're not independent enough. In most other parts of the world, however, young adults are expected to maintain very close ties with their parents. Striving for autonomy is viewed as disrespectful.

This difference in world views often creates challenges when parents have recently immigrated to the United States from a country in which "interdependence," not independence, is prized, as it is in most Asian and Latinx societies. If the young adult grew up in the United States, they and their parents likely have very different ideas about what to expect from each other. Parents may be bothered and saddened by the fact that their adult child is so much more distant than they were from their own parents at the same age. They interpret this distance as a sign of impertinence or ingratitude when it's merely a reflection of the different perspectives on family relationships that they and their Americanized child have.

By the same token, a young adult who believes that independence is crucial to forming an adult identity may view their immigrant parents as overly intrusive and manipulative. Relative to their friends from nonimmigrant families, they see themselves as far more devoted to their parents—and they may actually *be* more devoted—and can't understand why their parents don't recognize and applaud this.

The different generations in new immigrant families are using different criteria to judge their relationship. The parents compare how their young adult treats them with how they treated their own parents, and they find their child lacking. The young adult compares how they treat their parents with the way their friends treat theirs, though. They view themselves as exceeding reasonable expectations for how a child should treat their mother and father.

If this sounds like your family, try discussing the situation with your child in a nonaccusatory fashion, without attempting to make them feel guilty about their behavior. Say something like "I understand that in this country, children aren't expected to treat their parents the way your father and I were raised to treat ours. But it's been hard for us to adjust to this. I wonder if we can find some middle ground between the two extremes." Be clear about what you expect, but be kind when describing how you'd like your child to act. "We care about you a lot—that's why we'd like to hear from you every day, to make sure things are going well. It's probably more than your friends' parents expect, but it would make us so happy. It's important to us that we have a close family." And try to understand that your child is influenced by the cultural context in which they've grown up, even if it isn't one you approve of.

❧

At the other end of the spectrum are parents who wish their adult kid would be *more* independent. This often happens when a young adult's self-doubt increases their dependence on their parents. Jenna, a thirty-three-year-old who had moved to Houston after she graduated college, was used to calling her parents in Chicago a few times each week to catch up. But soon after she and her boyfriend split up, she started calling them almost every day.

At first, her parents assumed it was because she was lonely. But as the calls continued, they noticed that she was increasingly asking their advice on what seemed like trivial matters. She texted them images of dishes she was thinking of buying and asked their opinion. She asked them whether she should switch cell phone plans. Her parents began to worry something was wrong. Instead of becoming more autonomous as she got older, Jenna was becoming more dependent. If this dynamic goes on too long, a vicious cycle can develop—the more the young person comes to depend on their parents, the shakier their self-confidence becomes, which only leads to further dependence.

When this pattern persisted for several months, her mother, Danielle, talked to her husband, Jeff, about it.

"I don't think it's normal," Danielle said as they sipped their tea one night after Jenna sought their counsel on what color to paint her bedroom. "Most of our friends complain that they don't know enough about their kids' lives. I know it sounds cold, but I wish we knew less, not more. Someone Jenna's age shouldn't be relying on her parents for advice about every decision they make."

Jeff disagreed. "I don't know," he said. "Shouldn't we be there for her? If your kid needs help, how can you say no? She did just break things off with Cameron. Maybe she needs to bounce decisions off us because she doesn't have him."

"I'm not saying we should say no," Danielle replied. "I'm just wondering whether it's more than that—if she's regressing, becoming more reliant on us when she should be becoming more independent."

If this describes your child, you need to decide whether their dependence is due to temporary circumstances or to something else, like depression or severe anxiety, both of which can make someone indecisive. Someone who's just ended a serious relationship, for example, may have grown accustomed to discussing their decisions with their partner. They're used to talking through things with someone who knows them well and whose advice they value. They may also have lost some friends after they and their partner broke up, because some of the people they had socialized with found it hard to remain friends with both of them. When young adults are newly single, they may feel a little rudderless and turn to their parents to fill this role.

If you sense your child's dependence on you will wane over time, you probably don't need to worry about it. When they come to you for advice, give it in a way that reassures them that they're competent and capable of running their own life. Say something like "I'm sure it's unfamiliar to be making a lot of decisions by yourself after you've been in a serious relationship." But don't make decisions for them. Instead, ask questions that will lead them to make up their mind.

Jenna's father suggested they try this approach. His wife agreed to go along with it, but insisted that if nothing changed after a month, they would need to speak to Jenna candidly about the situation.

Each time she called asking for advice, instead of giving it, Jeff or Danielle—whoever answered the phone—would ask pointed questions and reinforce Jenna's answers, whether they agreed or not. They correctly decided it was more important to make Jenna feel confident about her ability to make decisions than to express their own opinions.

When Jenna called one evening to ask whether they thought it was a good idea for her to get a dog, Danielle turned the question back to her.

"Do you think you'll have time to train it?" Danielle asked.

"I'm thinking about getting an older one, one that's already housebroken," Jenna said.

"Good idea. What about exercise?" Danielle asked. "Your apartment is pretty small."

"I thought about that," Jenna answered. "I've done some research, and I've narrowed it down to a French bulldog or a Pomeranian. According to what I've read, these are great breeds for people who live in apartments."

"Smart," Danielle said. "Sounds like you know what you're doing."

"I guess so. I've spent a lot of time online. And I called my friend's cousin, who's a vet. She was super helpful. I just wanted your opinion before I made a final decision."

"You know what, sweetie? You know a lot more about this than I do. I think you should follow your instincts. They're usually good."

After Jeff and Danielle stuck to this strategy consistently for several weeks, Jenna's requests for advice became less frequent. By reinforcing her competence, they helped build her confidence. Soon enough, she began calling to tell them about decisions she'd made rather than asking for their input.

On the other hand, if your kid's dependence has no obvious cause, you might ask a couple of friends who have a child the same age as yours if their child behaves similarly. You may discover that your child's reliance on you isn't unusual—as I've explained, this generation of young adults is much more used to discussing every-day things with their parents than you were at the same age. How-ever, if you're concerned that the dependence is due to insecurity or a lack of confidence, and you're close enough to your child to probe a bit, you should talk about it. If your child is depressed or unduly anxious, counseling might be in order (see chapter 3, "Getting Help" on page 62).

❧

It's more common for young adults to question their parents' opinion than to seek it, though, and to rely on their friends' advice instead. If given the choice, your adult child might prefer to sit in a room they know isn't as pleasing as it might have been with your input, know-ing that they picked the colors and furnishings themselves. They'll derive more satisfaction from knowing they addressed the problem with their office mate without your guidance, even if the solution is imperfect. Your child will always look at the dresser as something that they built, even if it isn't quite level.

Your child needs to show you, and themselves, that they can decorate an apartment, solve an office problem, or follow a set of instructions without you. And now your child knows that they're competent enough to be an adult on their own—and what a great feeling that is! Don't diminish this sense of accomplishment because your feelings are hurt or because you could have helped prevent some mistakes. It's more important that you not let your feelings in the moment hamper their long-term growth.

And it is essential that you refrain from comparing their transition into adulthood with your own.

## "When I Was Your Age"

There are certain expressions to avoid when talking to your grown child. Perhaps the most offensive is "When I was your age." You certainly were once your child's age, but you didn't grow up in the same era they did, and that makes any comparison to their situation specious. Being twenty, or thirty, or even forty today isn't the same as it was when you were a young adult—just as those ages were different for you than they were for your parents.

"When I was your age" is almost always said in a deprecating way, an insinuation that your child's accomplishments are less than yours when you were their age. You were married rather than single. Living in a four-bedroom house with a backyard rather than a two-room walk-up in a dicey neighborhood—or a childhood bedroom. Raising a happy brood of children rather than being childless. Halfway up the career ladder rather than on the second rung. Owning a handsome savings account rather than living paycheck to paycheck. Financially self-sufficient rather than needing to borrow money from your parents sometimes.

Saying, "When I was your age" to a young adult is akin to saying, "Don't talk back" to a four-year-old, "Children should be seen and not heard" to an eight-year-old, "You'll know better when you grow up" to a twelve-year-old, or "If I want your opinion I'll ask for it" to a sixteen-year-old. These expressions are all insulting and disrespectful. If you want your grown child to respect you, you need to respect them.

The two biggest external factors that distinguish your child's generation from yours are changes in the world of work and the cost of housing. The labor force has been transformed in myriad ways that no one could have anticipated thirty years ago. The amount of education needed to be competitive in the job market is far greater now than a generation ago. Old jobs disappear and new, even unimagined, ones emerge in the blink of an eye. People's skills become outdated and the demands placed on them to acquire new skills intensify. Even before the pandemic, boundaries between home and work were eroding. A deluge of work email that arrived overnight greets the morning. Success requires a willingness to toil at all hours, including weekends.

And then there's housing. The cost of buying a home has risen far faster than the rate of inflation. In the last decade alone, the median cost of housing in the United States has risen by about 30 percent, whereas average salaries have risen by just 10 percent. In the last fifty years, even after adjusting for inflation, the average price of a home rose five times faster than the average salary. Is it any surprise that many young couples need help from their parents for a down payment?

As we saw earlier in this chapter, the entire timetable of young adulthood has changed radically. A generation ago, it would have been reasonable to expect a thirty-year-old to be married and to have started a family. Today, at least for college-educated people, much less those who continued their education beyond college, this expectation just isn't realistic.

If you still can't shake the "When I was your age" mentality, subtract at least five years from your age before you make the comparison. That is, if your kid is thirty-five years old, compare their position in life now to where you were when thirty, because the transition to adulthood now occurs five years later than a generation ago.

You might end up using "When I was your age" to mean that you weren't nearly as accomplished as they are when you were their age.

## CHAPTER TWO

# Growing Together

## To Bite, or Not to Bite

One of the most common questions parents ask me is "When should I bite my tongue, and when should I speak up?" If you're the parent of an adult child, you probably bite your tongue a lot. And you probably wonder each time whether you should have kept your mouth shut or spoken up.

Parents have different philosophies about how often and under what circumstances they should speak their mind. They also differ as to how to express themselves when they choose to speak up. I've heard parents describe two extreme philosophies, both of which are problematic.

One school of thought says that parents should always keep their mouths shut. According to this perspective, you're asking for trouble by speaking up, because even though your child is still your child, they're an adult, and they're entitled to live their life as they please. This approach sounds fine in theory, but it doesn't make a lot of sense in practice. After all, you have close friends who also are adults, and you probably speak candidly to them when you're concerned they might be making a serious mistake. What sort of person stands idly by while their friend makes a terrible decision? By the same logic, why shouldn't you give your kid your honest opinion? Even if you think that supporting your kid's autonomy is important, there no doubt are situations in which voicing legitimate concerns about their well-being is paramount.

If you're worried they'll get angry at you for speaking up, ask yourself three things:

- Is your relationship so fragile that you can't openly disagree about anything consequential?
- Do the benefits of speaking up outweigh the costs of keeping your mouth shut?
- How will walking on eggshells around your child affect your own mental health? You'll feel better if you speak up and your child doesn't follow your advice than if you don't and feel like a misunderstood martyr.

You've probably heard stories of parents whose adult child cut them out of their life because of some innocuous comment the parents made. But, according to rigorous studies, this sort of permanent estrangement is very rare. And I doubt such an excessive reaction is ever prompted by one misinterpreted remark. If it appears to be, something else unacknowledged may be going on, like long-term unvoiced resentment, which you and your kid should discuss (see "Handling Your Own Unpleasant Emotions" on page 35).

❧

The other extreme is the belief that you should always tell your child when you disagree with them. The logic behind this stance is that, as a parent, you're not only entitled to express your opinions, you're *obliged* to. Part of your role is to protect your child from harm—this is always how you've behaved, and you see no reason to change course now.

You know your child is entitled to live their life as they wish and make their own mistakes. But you also know that you're older, wiser, and more experienced than they are. How can you bite your tongue when you're sure (or pretty sure) your child will look back on their decision with regret?

The problem is that speaking your mind whenever you like directly clashes with the young person's need for autonomy, a collision that will often make your child defensive and perhaps distant.

Although you may have spoken up out of genuine concern for your kid's well-being, they may not always view it this way. Adult children often are still struggling with their own desire to see themselves, and be seen, as capable, fully competent adults—which in many ways they probably are. Regardless of how well-meaning you are (and regardless of how obvious you think your intentions are), your criticism can trigger your child's self-doubt, inadequacy, or embarrassment.

These uncomfortable feelings may make your child angry—not so much at you for the criticism, but at themselves for doing whatever you criticized. But because we don't like feeling angry at ourselves at any age, we often turn that anger outward, toward the most convenient target. And because your remark set this whole process in motion, that target will likely be you. Your child may not even understand this—they may say to themselves or their partner or friends, "I don't know why my parents make me feel this way; they just do."

I know this explanation is cold comfort. Even if you realize what's going on in your child's head, it's only natural to feel hurt when something you said or did out of heartfelt concern is taken as inconsiderate and intrusive.

Telling your child, "I was only trying to help" may smooth things over occasionally (if your child's wound isn't very deep or if they're especially secure), but if you say it too often, it will fall on deaf ears. This is why always speaking up can be bad for you, your child, and your relationship.

Each of these extreme positions falls short because it applies a rigid rule. Blindly following a set doctrine is certainly easy, because it saves you the hassle of having to really think about the right response to each situation. But your goal as a parent shouldn't be keeping things simple. Just accept that you must make tough, careful decisions about whether or not to bite your tongue. Being a good parent was hard work when your child was younger, and it still is.

Let this principle guide you when you seek to navigate between those dangerous extremes: *Speak up when you must, but unless your child specifically asks for it, keep your opinion to yourself.*

Allowing them to make a mistake that won't have dire consequences is more important than your being correct. If you follow this maxim consistently you'll likely find that your child asks for your opinion more and more over time.

There are three things to consider when deciding whether speaking up is a "must":

First, is your child about to do something that could have harmful and perhaps long-term consequences they haven't considered? It's true that children, even adult children, benefit by learning from their mistakes. But not all mistakes are benign, and some of the lessons come at a steep cost. Marrying someone with a history of domestic violence is dangerous. Investing money earmarked for a down payment on a house in a speculative "sure thing" is a bad idea. Quitting a job impulsively without having adequate savings or a new job lined up isn't prudent. Speak up if you have legitimate reason to be seriously concerned, and make sure to explain yourself without lecturing or implying that your child is foolish or too young to know better. "I know the preschool you're leaning toward is convenient, but the way you described it concerns me. They shouldn't be assigning 'homework' to three-year-olds. Experts say that, at this age, children learn best through play."

Second, recognize that your disagreement could be one of opinion rather than substance. You think your child should rent the roomier of two apartments they're considering; they want the one in the building with more amenities. Your child and their partner may have a different approach to parenting than you and your spouse did; trends in parenting advice, just like trends in footwear, food, and furniture, change with the times (see chapter 8, "Giving Advice About Your Child's Parenting" on page 201). What was considered the "right" way to raise a child when you were a young parent may no longer be in vogue or recommended by pediatricians. (Decades of research on family relationships, including my own studies, show that minor variations in parenting practices probably don't matter as much as their proponents insist they do.) Save your opinions for issues that really matter. That way, when you do speak up, your child will be more likely to pay attention. They won't always heed your advice, but there's a better chance they'll consider it.

Third, ask yourself if you're disagreeing over something in which you have special expertise. If you're a building contractor, you probably know better than your child what to look for when touring homes for sale. If you're an interior designer, you probably know where to find the best prices for sofas or stoves. If you're an elementary school teacher, you probably know a lot about teaching a child how to read. If you're wavering between giving or withholding advice, I'd lean toward speaking up if your professional knowledge can help forestall a disastrous home purchase, save your child some money, help your grandchild develop important skills, or contribute to your child's welfare in some other consequential way.

Before you express a difference of opinion on something consequential, think about the best way to express yourself. Try to avoid directives ("Don't waste your money on that"), remarks that might be interpreted as insulting ("You never had a good eye for design"), comments that could exacerbate conflict between your child and their partner ("I know you two disagree, but you're simply right about this one"), or framing issues in catastrophic terms ("Believe me, you'll regret this decision").

A far better approach is to frame your opinion in the form of a question designed to help your child think through the matter more rigorously than they may have as of yet ("I understand why you like this car, but have you thought about whether taking out a large auto loan right now might make you lose sleep about money?") or as a request for information ("I don't know much about induction cooktops other than that they're quite expensive. Can you explain why people think they're better than gas ones?"). Gently prodding your child to think about or explain their reasoning may end up changing their opinion, or yours—either of which will temper any dispute without hurting anyone's feelings.

However you approach this, if you had bitten your tongue and your child made a decision that turned out poorly, don't say you knew they were making a bad decision all along but decided to keep your mouth shut. Your child will probably wonder—and may even ask—why you didn't speak up at the time. (I know, I know, sometimes you just can't win.) If you spoke up, but your child disregarded your advice and ended up regretting their decision, don't remind them that you had warned them. And if your advice proved correct and your child is in a tough spot because they ignored it, help remedy the problem or bail your child out if you can, without rubbing it in. No one likes to hear "I told you so," especially from a parent.

If you've always been quick to offer assistance or support before your child asks, it will probably feel unnatural to wait for their request now. But holding back is its own form of help. You're encouraging their autonomy and independence, which is exactly what they need at this age.

Still, you may feel anxious about being less forthcoming with your support. Will your kid feel like you're cutting them off? But if you've been protective throughout their childhood and adolescence, I doubt they'll think you've suddenly stopped caring about them. Frankly, they probably know exactly what you're doing, even if they might not realize how hard it is for you. And if they want your advice, they'll ask for it.

Feeling guilty or irritated for biting your tongue are just two of many uncomfortable emotions this stage of parenting may evoke. Uncomfortable feelings don't necessarily mean you've done something wrong. Many times, they're just a signal that you're doing things differently. Unfamiliar behavior can be uncomfortable. The challenge is figuring out how best to ease your discomfort.

## Handling Your Own Unpleasant Emotions

Just because your kid is now an adult doesn't mean that they stop annoying you or letting you down sometimes. You've taken a lot of time to find the perfect gift for them, but they don't seem to appreciate your effort. You feel like they only call when they need something from you. They knew you had a doctor's appointment, but they forgot to ask you how it went. They got a promotion, but you learned about it secondhand when one of their friend's parents called you with congratulations.

Every so often you'll feel unappreciated, taken for granted, neglected, or mistreated. These emotions are understandable, and you shouldn't feel bad for having them. The question is how to best handle them. Do you brush them off and try to forget about them? Ponder them for a while until they cease to bother you? Stew about them for some time? Discuss them with your partner or a friend? Or tell your child how you feel?

The answer depends on three things: your temperament, the seriousness of the slight, and, most important, how often these sorts of things happen.

Some of us are naturally more inclined to ruminate about things that annoy us. We replay events in our mind and imagine how much better we would have felt if things had gone differently. How nice it would have been to see your child's face when they opened your gift, or to tell your friend how proud you felt when you heard about the promotion a few days ago. Sometimes we can't help playing things over and over in our minds, but studies have found that rumination tends to make us feel worse, not better, so if you can avoid or limit this behavior, your mental health will thank you. Try meditating or changing your focus instead of ruminating.

The impact of discussing a bothersome event with a partner or friend depends on whether the conversation helps you think about it in a less negative light or whether it devolves into what psychologists call "co-rumination"—when you do your stewing out loud and the listener mainly empathizes. This, too, has been the subject of psychological study, and the results show that co-rumination is sometimes worse for your well-being than ruminating alone (it's not so good for the co-ruminator, either). True, misery loves company, but it usually makes us feel even more miserable after the company has left. If you want to discuss the situation, choose someone who's likely to make you feel less irritated about the situation, somebody who's good at helping you see things more objectively. You probably already know who in your inner circle are good at this.

Other people are more temperamentally inclined to do just the opposite—to not give the event much thought or to persuade themselves that they overreacted. The costs and benefits of these strategies depend in part on whether you're accepting the feeling and moving on, which is fine, or whether you're denying the feeling, which isn't. Refusing to accept unpleasant feelings takes a fair amount of emotional energy, and doing so too often can be draining. It's far better to acknowledge the feeling, understand its origins, and figure out what you might do to avoid feeling this way in the future. Perhaps you had unreasonably high expectations that contributed to your reaction. If so, you can lower them (see chapter 1, "Adjusting Your Expectations" on page 11).

The hardest decision is whether to say anything about the event to your child. Here's where it's important to take into account the severity and frequency of the event. If they forgot to call and ask about a doctor's appointment, you should let this slide, or perhaps say something like "I can't recall if I told you, but I had my appointment with my cardiologist today and everything is fine." If they forgot to ask about the outcome of a more serious procedure, it's quite reasonable to say something like "I'm surprised you didn't phone to ask about the angioplasty. I told you that I had to spend the night in the hospital, didn't I?"

As for frequency, it's wise to speak up if the same sort of inconsideration happens regularly. There's no magic number by which to define "regularly," but it's important to say something before you begin to feel resentful. Once that sets in, you may stop doing the things you believe are taken for granted, or lower your expectations so much that you pull back a bit from the relationship. The danger here is a vicious cycle, in which you and your child grow increasingly distant. You can short-circuit this by saying to them, "You know, I've been feeling somewhat unappreciated and neglected, kind of taken for granted. Not all the time, but often enough that I had to say something about it."

They will likely be surprised and apologetic. If they ask you to enumerate all of the ways in which they've disappointed you, say something like "I haven't kept a list, but please just accept my feeling that it's been frequent enough that I needed to tell you."

You might end the conversation by saying that if they ever feel similarly about you—that you weren't grateful for something they did, misunderstood something they said, or weren't included in something they think they should have been—you'd like them to tell you rather than hold their feelings in.

We all have idiosyncrasies that sometimes get in the way of our relationships. You've learned by now that there are things you do that push your kid's buttons, and you probably try to avoid pushing them. But maybe you haven't spent enough time thinking about your own buttons, and what your child unknowingly does to push them.

It's a natural human tendency to attribute other people's overreactions to their inherent shortcomings while viewing our own intense emotions as entirely rational. We blame other people's behavior on their personality, but explain our own behavior as an unavoidable consequence of our situation.

Like everyone else, you have your issues. You may not be able to rid yourself of them, but being aware of what involuntarily aggravates you will go a long way toward having a better relationship with your child (and, for that matter, with anyone).

Call them whatever you want—pet peeves, trigger points, sore spots, neuroses—but everybody has them. We aren't always aware of them, but they're often obvious to those who know us well. When others point them out, sometimes we admit to them sheepishly, sometimes we do so grudgingly, sometimes we justify them, and sometimes we outright deny them (ironically, refusing to acknowledge our own shortcomings is a fairly common shortcoming).

Some of us are hypersensitive to criticism, whereas others are hypercritical (these often go hand in hand). Some of us are suspicious, others guileless. Some are excessively bothered by clutter, while others are uncannily oblivious to it. Some people are frugal, but others are spendthrifts. Some people are easily wounded, some carry around grudges beyond their expiration date; some can't apologize when they're wrong, and others demand being apologized to more regretfully than is necessary. Some people can't stand being argued with; others get annoyed when people won't engage them in a debate.

Many of these traits are so common that psychologists have invented jargon to describe them. A lot of people are prone to "negative affectivity," a heightened tendency to experience unpleasant emotions, like sadness, anger, or anxiety. Some of us are high in "rejection sensitivity," a proneness to look for, and find, signs that others don't like us.

I don't think it's all that valuable to try to understand the origins of these sore spots, nor is there much evidence that figuring out their root causes makes them go away. But being aware of what easily activates these gut responses is important.

The outcome of an interaction between any two people is often the product of the unspoken (and sometimes unconscious) expectations, biases, and habits each of them brings to the situation. After some soul-searching, you may see that the main cause of a problem between you and your kid has something to do with *your* issues, which color how you interpret your child's behavior.

Before you jump to the conclusion that your child has hurt you, stop and check your own emotional baggage. Ask yourself if you're being overly sensitive or unduly defensive. Sometimes, these wounds are self-inflicted. Remember, it takes two to tangle. That's why it's crucial to learn how to resolve conflicts in ways that solve, rather than exacerbate, the problem.

## Resolving Disputes Constructively

Everyone understands the negative aspects of conflict, but we tend to forget the positive ones. Conflict prods us into expressing, rather than suppressing, our feelings. It shocks us out of our passivity, forcing us to think about what we've taken for granted, change our ways, and solve our problems. Going through life avoiding conflict confines us to superficial relationships and psychological stagnation.

You probably had plenty of disagreements with your teenager—arguments between parents and their children peak soon after puberty. Although the frequency and intensity of such conflicts will probably decline over time, they won't disappear. Even after you've resolved some issues, new ones will arise as you discover differences of opinion over matters you'd never had to deal with before. Until now, you and your kid never tangled over how best to finance the purchase of a home, allocate holiday time between your family and their partner's, or raise children.

Conflicts between parents and their adult children can arise for several reasons: when one of you feels that the other is threaten-

ing their values, perceptions, lifestyle, sense of fairness, or "terri-
tory"; when you and they agree on a final goal but disagree on how
to get there; when there's not enough of something to go around
(that "something" may be tangible, like money or space, or intan-
gible, like time, attention, or affection); and when communication
between the two of you has broken down.

When it's done right, conflict can improve all of these situations. It can invigorate a relationship by helping people understand
each other better, leading them to clarify issues in a way that reduces
tension, and forcing them to set new goals that are more satisfactory
to all concerned. However, conflict can harm a relationship when
it takes the form of personal attacks and power struggles. Negative
conflict leads to resentment and hostility; causes confusion, insecurity, and diminished self-esteem; and makes productive, rational
discussion of issues and behavior in the future difficult, if not impossible. When you and your child are at war, nobody wins.

❧

The four most common ways parents and children try to resolve
conflicts are refusing to back down, giving in, avoiding the problem, and compromise. Although each of these strategies has its
uses, each also has drawbacks. Let's see how each of these common
approaches plays out in the following scenario, which often arises
when a couple must figure out how to allocate holiday time between
their two families.

Before they married, Jay and Michael each spent Thanksgiving
with their extended family—grandparents, aunts and uncles, cousins, and the like. Even after they had gotten engaged, they still spent
the holiday apart, usually getting together on the weekend after the
celebration. Jay and Michael live in Chicago, and their families live

in Milwaukee and Madison, respectively. Each family lives in a home that hasn't enough space to accommodate everyone's extended family overnight.

In late October, Jay and his mother have an angry argument about where he and Michael will spend their first Thanksgiving as a married couple. Jay's mother insists that he spend Thanksgiving with them, and that she will prepare the same traditional meal she has done every year since Jay was a child. Michael is welcome to join them, she says, but the family isn't ending a thirty-year tradition just because their son got married. Here are several possible ways things might unfold:

*Refusing to back down.* Jay's mother refuses to consider any alternatives. Jay tells her she is being stubborn and inconsiderate, but she won't back down. He is furious.

*Giving in.* Jay tells Michael he doesn't see a solution other than just giving in. Michael tells Jay he will accompany him to Jay's parents' house and explain this year's conflict to his own parents, but that he and Jay will need to find a better solution next year. They end up going to Jay's parents' house grudgingly, but everyone around the table knows what happened, and things are awkward and uncomfortable. Thanksgiving at Michael's house without him present isn't a pleasant one for his family, either. Everyone's worried about whether future holidays will be problematic. And bad blood has now been spilled between the two sets of in-laws.

*Avoidance.* Jay tells Michael they should just avoid the situation—they'll have a quiet, romantic first Thanksgiving by themselves. But when they think about this, they realize this is just postponing the inevitable. Sooner or later, they're going to have to come up with a viable solution. It's clear to each of them that avoidance may solve things temporarily, but it doesn't resolve anything.

*Compromise.* "I have an idea," Michael says. "We'll have two

Thanksgiving meals," he tells Jay. "Lunch with your family and dinner with mine—or the opposite, whichever is easier."

"You know what's going to happen," Jay says. "Our parents will complain about who hosts lunch and who hosts dinner, and they'll both feel short-changed because our visits will be cut short. And you and I will spend seven hours in the car, ready to fall asleep on the highway from all the tryptophan and wine."

Most of us have been raised to think the best way to resolve a conflict is to compromise, but this isn't always the case. Compromise, it's been said, is just a way of ensuring that no one is entirely happy with the solution.

❧

There's a fifth approach that usually works better than any of the above: collaborative problem-solving.

The goal of collaborative problem-solving, which is common in business settings, is finding a solution that gives everyone some satisfaction. This approach takes more time and energy than the others I've described, but usually it minimizes hostility and hurt feelings and maximizes the chances you'll truly resolve the issue. It requires that the parties involved work together to come up with a solution that each can live with. Each party agrees to treat the other party with respect—no name-calling, sarcasm, or put-downs—and to listen to the other person's point of view. They brainstorm together and come up with a list of possible solutions without judging them. And then they honestly discuss the pros and cons of each.

Here's how it worked successfully for Jay and his mother:

Jay suggested that they try to work together to find a solution to their problem. He drove to her house in Milwaukee as a gesture of good faith, and she baked Jay's favorite cookies in return. Over warm cookies and several cups of tea, they came to understand that the best solution, at least for the time being, was to have two Thanksgiving meals, one on Thursday and one on Friday, and in the future to alternate from year to year which family hosted each. There was a guest room in each family's house where Jay and Michael could spend the night so that they wouldn't have to do so much driving in a single day. And after they returned home, Jay and Michael would go out for a private, romantic dinner back in Chicago, on Saturday night.

"Okay," Jay's mother said, "but who gets to have the 'real' Thanksgiving the first year?"

"You're joking, right?" Jay asked.

"Of course I am," she said, half meaning it. "But I think it's only fair that we get to have it, since I helped come up with the solution!"

Occasional disagreements with your adult child are inevitable. And so are disagreements with your partner about how to parent them.

## When You and Your Partner Disagree

The essential ingredients of jointly parenting an adult child successfully are fundamentally the same as when your child was younger: providing your partner with support, care, and assistance. The main source of difficulty is the same, too: dealing with differences of opinion over how to respond to an issue that concerns both of you. Of course, the issues themselves change over time.

Before your kids became adults, you didn't have to discuss whether to share your opinion about their choice of a potential spouse, how much financial help to give them, or whether to express your concerns over how they raise their children. As unexpected issues arise, you'll likely discover that you have differing views about how to handle them.

Your child's transition into adulthood may also change the dynamics of the joint and independent relationships you and your partner have with them. You probably discovered, as most couples do, that different stages of your child's development stimulated and supported different degrees and types of involvement from each of you. One of you loved seeing the preschool paintings displayed by your child and their classmates at back-to-school nights; the other had to feign delight. One of you was thrilled to coach your child's soccer team; the other couldn't have been less interested. One of you taught your teenager how to drive; the other was petrified at the mere prospect.

Because opportunities for engagement in your child's life will vary as they move into and through adulthood, some of these will just naturally appeal to you more than to your partner, and vice versa. It's good to try to take an interest in your adult child's interests, but it's fine if one of you is more inclined than the other to get involved. Do your best to avoid seeing these differences as indications of which parent your child prefers. Hopefully, they love and respect each of you for who you are and have been, not because one of you was more skilled at, or interested in, the activities that excited them at a particular time in their life.

Relationships among three people often have uncomfortable dynamics. You'll go through periods when you feel like the outsider, listening in on excited conversations between your child and your partner about topics that you have little interest in or knowledge about, and you'll discover that the two of them have talked about you in your absence. But there will be times in the future, as there were in the past, when the alliances will be reversed—when you'll be the more involved parent and your partner will feel left out.

Rather than feel sorry that you're an interloper at a party you weren't interested in attending in the first place, step back and admire your partner for the way they and your child bond over interests they share. Your separate relationships with your child don't amount to a zero-sum game. If you can keep feelings of jealousy and exclusion at bay, you'll see that strong ties between your child and your partner can strengthen, not undermine, your relationship with your kid. A secure parent feels pleasure, not envy, when watching their partner and their child having special times together. If seeing your kid and your partner enjoying themselves bugs you, you have yourself, not your partner, to blame.

❧

One question that often arises when parents disagree about how to treat their child is whether to present a united front. The older your child is, the less important this is. It makes sense to appear unified before they've reached adolescence, because younger children may find it unsettling and confusing otherwise. But by the time they're a teenager, they know that people in a close relationship often disagree. When we reach adolescence, we have the cognitive abilities necessary to understand that there's often more than one reasonable opinion on an issue.

Presenting a united front to an adult child is also pointless because by now they know who's usually the pushover on certain issues and who's more likely to hold their ground, so your child will easily see through any phony appearance of harmony. It's fine to say, "Your father and I don't see eye to eye about this, but we've decided that it's best to follow my instincts this time."

Handling disagreements with a partner that arise in a second (or third) marriage is trickier, because many of their opinions about parenting were established long before they became a stepparent. An approach that may seem perfectly reasonable to the child's parent may strike the stepparent as worrisome or, worse, unacceptable. As you might expect, this often happens when one of the parents has raised their children very permissively or very strictly, and the other came at parenting with the opposite philosophy.

This is the situation Peter and Maria found themselves in. They met in San Diego when they were in their fifties. Both had been married before and had children of their own. Maria's two daughters were in their early twenties, off at college. Peter's son and daughter had already graduated college and were living across the country.

After dating for a little over a year, Peter and Maria decided they would marry, sell their separate homes, pool the proceeds, and buy a house together. Not long after they moved in, Maria, Peter, and Maria's daughters went on a weeklong trip to visit Maria's sister and her husband in Arizona. It was Peter's first extended visit to a member of Maria's family.

The first night they were there, Maria's sister made dinner for the six of them. After everyone had finished, the two young women sat at the table, whispering with each other without even clearing their plates, much less offering to help with the dishes. Peter told Maria's sister and her husband to relax while he and Maria cleaned up the table and loaded the dishwasher. He was hoping this might goad his stepdaughters into helping, but it was to no avail. Although he was angry, he didn't want to make a scene.

When Peter and Maria got into bed that night, he was still annoyed. "They acted like entitled princesses," he complained. "It's not right, and you should say something to them about it in the morning. It's embarrassing. They ought to apologize."

"I'm not bothered by it," Maria replied, yawning. "They've always been that way. But as long as they do well in school and stay out of trouble, I'm happy."

Peter let it slide, hoping to avoid an argument. As he lay there, he convinced himself that they would probably become more considerate as they matured.

Nothing in the daughters' dinner table manners changed with time, however. Whenever the four of them were at family gatherings, the daughters—now in their mid-twenties—were just as inconsiderate as they had been when they were younger. Peter was now even more bothered by their behavior, given their ages.

One evening, after a holiday dinner with Peter's family, the young women repeated their typical after-dinner behavior. Peter once again expressed his annoyance to his wife, but Maria said there was nothing she, or anyone else, could do.

He didn't want to argue. As he drifted off to sleep, he accepted that Maria was probably right—trying to teach his stepdaughters manners wasn't likely to work. He also concluded that it wasn't his responsibility and that holding on to his anger about this might hurt his marriage. Although their poor manners continued to irk him, he didn't speak to Maria about it again.

Whether you're in your first marriage or a second or third one, it's important to remember when you're co-parenting that the two of you are partners. Managing your relationship with each other is just as important as managing your relationship with your child. Most of the time, when you and your partner have different opinions about a grown child's behavior, try to follow one of the three strategies I outlined earlier: compromise; allow the person with the most relevant experience to decide what's best; or have a friendly discussion, go with one person's plan, and agree to disagree.

## CHAPTER THREE

# Mental Health

## Young Adulthood Is a Vulnerable Period

Most serious mental health problems make their first appearance sometime between the ages of ten and twenty-five. This includes depressive disorders, anxiety disorders, substance use disorders, eating disorders, and conduct disorders, as well as psychotic disorders such as schizophrenia and bipolar disorder. The few disorders that typically appear before adolescence, such as autism spectrum disorder (ASD) or attention deficit hyperactivity disorder (ADHD), often persist into young adulthood.

Mental health problems are common during adulthood—in any given year, one-quarter of the U.S. adult population will suffer from a diagnosable mental disorder. But across all stages of development, adolescents and young adults are most vulnerable to mental health problems. In national surveys conducted before the COVID-19 pandemic (when rates of psychological problems increased markedly among all age groups), eighteen- to twenty-five-year-olds reported higher rates of psychological disorders than any other age group, in part because they continued to suffer from problems they've had since they were teenagers, and in part because they developed disorders for the first time, in their early twenties.

The prevalence of mental health problems among young people has risen dramatically in recent decades. According to annual surveys, rates of mental health disorders among people between the ages of eighteen and twenty-five increased substantially between 2008 and 2017. In one study, the percent of young adults who reported having had a major depressive episode in the month prior to the survey doubled over this ten-year period, whereas rates of major depressive episodes among adults in other age groups were unchanged.

People who report psychological distress far outnumber those who have a major clinical episode. In 2017, about 13 percent of young adults reported experiencing serious distress in the last month. This figure nearly doubled between 2008 and 2017. In contrast, rates of psychological distress rose only marginally during this time period among adults between the ages of twenty-six and forty-nine, and were unchanged among those fifty and older. Suicidal thinking rose dramatically among young adults ages eighteen to twenty-five as well, although there were substantial increases in suicidal ideation among people in their late twenties and early thirties, too.

We've all heard about the staggering increase in mental health problems that took place at all ages during the pandemic. The number of U.S. adults reporting symptoms of depression or anxiety increased from 11 percent before the pandemic to more than 40 percent during it. More than 13 percent of people reported an increase in substance use. When surveyed, more than 10 percent said they'd thought about suicide in the prior thirty days.

The pandemic took an especially severe toll on the psychological health of young adults. During the crisis, nearly two-thirds of people between the ages of eighteen and twenty-four reported symptoms of depression or anxiety, one-quarter reported an increase in their substance use as a means of coping with pandemic-related stress, and one-quarter reported seriously considering suicide.

By any indicator, whether before or after the pandemic, people in their late teens and early twenties are more likely to report serious mental health symptoms than any other adults. Those between the ages of twenty-five and forty are not far behind.

To understand why mental health problems are so common in young adulthood, it helps to look at the causes of psychological problems more generally.

Most psychological problems are due to the combination of an internal vulnerability and external stress. The internal vulnerability can be inborn (like inheriting a predisposition to addiction), acquired from prior experience (like abusive parenting), or neurodevelopmental (like being at an age when the brain is especially malleable). The external stress can be chronic (poverty) or acute (exposure to combat), biological (an illness) or nonbiological (job loss), interpersonal (a breakup) or situational (a hurricane), subjective (worrying that a blizzard may make you miss the last flight back home) or objective (sitting in the terminal overnight waiting for the airport to reopen).

Because psychological problems result from this interplay between internal vulnerability and external stress, people with different degrees of vulnerability (for instance, a stronger or weaker inborn tendency toward intense emotional reactions to unpleasant events) who are exposed to the same type and degree of stress (say, a local crime wave) won't be equally affected by the experience. The person with the reactive temperament may develop debilitating anxiety, whereas the more placid person may be unaffected. Keep this in mind before remarking that your child's response to a stressful event, like the end of a romance, is an overreaction. Given their temperament, it may not be.

By the same token, someone with an inherited predisposition to depression who grew up with very loving parents may never become depressed, while someone with the identical genetic vulnerability, but emotionally abusive parents, will be far more likely to develop the disorder. This helps explain why rates of anxiety rose dramatically during the pandemic in general without impairing everyone's mental health. The pandemic was objectively stressful for millions of people, but some of them were protected by the good fortune of having hardier genes.

With all these factors in mind, it isn't hard to see why young adults face such an elevated risk for mental health problems. The brain's heightened plasticity, which I discussed earlier, makes people this age more susceptible to their environment. It makes them more likely to benefit from positive experiences, but more likely to be harmed by negative ones. This is one reason that young people were most adversely affected by the pandemic.

Even without a pandemic, the sheer number of environmental stresses young people face—more than any age group—makes them more susceptible than others to mental distress.

It's a time when people graduate from high school and transition into college, often moving out of their parents' home and leaving important relationships behind. Living away at college is a liberating experience for many, but a terrifying one for others. College may bring new academic demands that far exceed those faced in high school.

And completing college, especially these days, often carries great uncertainty about the future—about a job, living arrangements, finances, and a love life—not to mention paying off student debt, applying to graduate or professional school, or having to move home.

As far as we know, the brain's heightened plasticity during this period of life has always existed—long before scientists had the tools to discover and document it. Human evolution over millions of years made the young adult brain especially reactive to environmental conditions to help people acquire useful new knowledge about the world before venturing out on their own. As I noted earlier, however, this sensitivity also makes the young adult brain especially vulnerable to stress. The heightened stress responsivity probably hasn't changed in recent decades—far too short a period of time to be affected by evolution.

It's far more plausible that young adulthood has simply become more stressful, particularly in recent decades, as a consequence of an uncertain economy, the competitiveness of admission to selective colleges, a challenging labor market, the increased cost of housing and education, and excessive attention to social media. Many young people today also feel an existential anxiety fostered by climate change, cultural and political divisiveness, frightening international conflicts, rising gun violence, and the possibility that pandemics may become a permanent part of life. If we'd like to reverse the worrisome increases that have taken place in the last two decades in depression, anxiety, and suicidal thinking among young people, we must find ways of making young adulthood less stressful.

☙

Parents can do four things to help protect their adult children from developing a serious mental health problem—but keep in mind that you can do everything in your control and still not successfully prevent it. The extent to which parents can do any of these things will vary depending on whether the child is still at home, away at college, or living on their own, but in all these cases parents can take steps to make this time less stressful for their kids.

First, we must provide love, support, and reassurance. Many people don't realize how important being a warm and connected parent is to the mental health of their adult children. Knowing you're able to turn to your parents for emotional support is especially critical during transitions that may make young people anxious, like graduating from college, searching for a job, or moving to a new location. Keep in mind that these transitions can be both sources of excitement and worry, and it's possible you might not notice your child's anxiety if they only talk to you about what they're looking forward to, or if the positive aspects of their new life are all you ever ask about. It's fine to say, "These are big changes for you— how are you holding up?"

Young adults also need to know they can turn to their parents before, during, and after distressing events, such as the loss of a job, a friend's overdose, or a breakup. Sometimes these things happen without warning, but often there are signals—their employer has been laying off coworkers for a month, their friend has been grappling with a substance abuse problem for some time, their relationship has been on the rocks for the past year. These sorts of negative experiences can be stressful at any point in life, but their impact is magnified when the brain is especially sensitive to stress.

Ask your child how they're handling these situations and assure them of your willingness to talk any time. You can broach the subject by saying something like "You mentioned last week you were nervous about all the layoffs at work. How are you doing?" Even if they don't take you up on your offer to talk, just knowing you're there is an important comfort. And it's fine for you to check in every once in a while during especially difficult times (but not so often that it becomes intrusive) to see how they're faring. Pay attention to signals that you're being too nosy. For example, when otherwise talkative kids feel a parent is being intrusive, they clam up.

Second, try to minimize stresses in your child's life that can increase the likelihood that they'll develop a mental health problem. These might include giving or lending them money during a challenging financial time; sending them a gift certificate for a massage if they've been working especially hard; providing babysitting so they can have a relaxing night out; or treating them to something special that may distract them from their difficulties, like tickets to the theater or a sporting event, or a weekend getaway. If you yourself are a source of stress, do something to mitigate that. They don't need to hear about your own problems at work or conflicts with friends, or your "organ recitals"—the litany of complaints about the infirmities that often accompany getting older.

Third, help your child manage stress. There isn't much they can do about an overly critical boss, a colicky baby, or a landlord who promises to fix things but never does. But there are healthy and unhealthy ways of coping with stress. Gently suggest that they make time to exercise, sleep, eat well, and practice yoga, meditation, or progressive muscle relaxation, all of which reduce stress. (These techniques are effective at any age, so if you're stressed out about anything—including your kid—they'd be valuable for you, too.) If you think your child is turning to alcohol or other drugs as a means of coping, say something about it: "I've noticed that you've been drinking more than usual ever since things got more demanding around the office. What about going for a run after work to unwind after a long day once in a while instead of pouring a glass of wine?"

Fourth, tell your child about any vulnerabilities that they might not know about, such as a history of substance abuse or depression in the family. Most mental illnesses have at least some genetic component, and your child deserves to know whether they might be susceptible to addiction or another disorder. You may feel hesitant to share that one of your grandparents was an alcoholic, your uncle committed suicide, or you and your brother both take antidepressant medication, but your discomfort shouldn't stop you from sharing important information that may help your kid make better decisions about their own health. If you knew they may have inherited a predisposition to skin cancer, you'd surely mention it to them and stress the importance of using sunscreen and minimizing sun exposure. You should take the same approach to mental illness.

Rather than raising the subject out of the blue, look for opportunities to bring it up, like news about a celebrity who sought treatment for drug abuse or committed suicide. This can be an awkward subject for parents to raise—especially when you feel like you're divulging a family secret or breaking a confidence—but you can explain that this isn't information to be casually shared with others. Your child will likely understand and appreciate the fact that you view them as mature enough to entrust with this information.

## Common Mental Health Problems

Clinicians typically use the word "disorder" to describe serious mental health problems, like depressive disorders or substance abuse disorders. Technically, a "disorder" refers to a clinical diagnosis with a specific set of symptoms that persist for a particular period of time and that impair functioning in social relationships, school, work, or daily life. In other words, a disorder means that someone not only has certain symptoms, but that the symptoms aren't transitory and impair their functioning in one or more realms of their life.

Here I'm using the word "disorder" more broadly, to include both clinically defined disorders and conditions that don't necessarily meet the criteria for a formal diagnosis. It's possible to get little pleasure out of life without suffering from clinical depression or to worry all the time without meeting the criteria for an anxiety disorder. Some people are abnormally preoccupied with their weight but don't have an eating disorder. Some people misuse drugs without having a substance abuse disorder.

When I discuss young adults with problems like depression, anxiety, bulimia, or substance abuse, I mean that they have psychological difficulties that are more worrisome than short-term feelings of sadness after a breakup, anxiety about a new job, worries that their clothes might make them look fat, or social drinking with friends on Saturday nights. The important issue is whether these difficulties are frequent enough to get in the way of normal functioning. That's what you should focus on if you're worried about your child's mental health.

Just because someone doesn't meet the clinical criteria for a particular disorder doesn't mean they don't have problems that merit serious attention. Although feeling sad doesn't by itself warrant a diagnosis of depression, some people feel so sad so often that they would benefit from treatment. Some walk around in a constant state of anxiety that makes it impossible for them to relax. Some worry too much about their weight and want to stop their unhealthy dieting. Some think they're getting high too often and need help cutting back or getting sober. In other words, it's appropriate to get help for a psychological problem even if it's not a diagnosable disorder.

If your adult child seems to be suffering from any of the problems I mentioned above for more than a couple of weeks, I highly recommend you consider whether some sort of professional treatment is necessary. Don't worry about trying to make an informal diagnosis. Many different problems share similar symptoms (for example, sleep problems are common consequences of many psychological conditions), and many people suffer from more than one condition at the same time. For example, people who are abnormally preoccupied with their weight are often depressed, people who abuse drugs are often anxious, and people who are depressed frequently experience extreme bouts of anxiety. If you're concerned about your child and want to describe their mental state to your physician in order to get a referral, just describe their symptoms, how long they've had them, and how they seem to be affecting their life.

The most common psychological problems among young adults are depression, anxiety, eating disorders, ADHD, and substance abuse. These are all treatable, generally with a combination of medication and psychotherapy.

*Depression.* Although people often use this term interchangeably with sadness, depression is more than sadness. It has emotional symptoms, including dejection, decreased enjoyment of pleasurable activities, and low self-esteem. It has cognitive symptoms, such as pessimism and hopelessness. It has motivational symptoms, including apathy and boredom. Finally, it often has physical symptoms, such as a loss of appetite, difficulty sleeping, and low energy. Depression is more common among young women than young men, but plenty of young adult men are depressed.

For some people, depression is a chronic illness that comes and goes over a period of years, although it rarely disappears for more than two months at a time. People with symptoms of chronic depression often have difficulty feeling pleasure from activities they had enjoyed in the past, and are sometimes described as being gloomy or emotionally flat. In some cases, depression can become so intense that it triggers thoughts of death or suicide. Anytime someone says they're thinking about killing themselves, don't leave them alone. Call 911 or take them to the closest emergency room.

*Anxiety.* Everyone feels anxious sometimes. Feeling nervous or fearful is a normal response to a frightening or threatening situation. It's not unusual to feel anxious when a hurricane is approaching, you hear a suspicious noise late at night, or you learn that you have COVID-19. Usually, these anxieties wane when the threat passes. But when feelings of anxiety are severe or frequent enough to interfere with day-to-day functioning, it may be time to seek professional help.

Generally, an expert will diagnose an anxiety disorder when someone has intense fears and worries that won't go away. Anxiety disorders are often accompanied by fatigue, sleep problems, and physical signs of tension, like headaches or stomachaches. The most common forms of anxiety in young adulthood are *generalized anxiety* (frequent worrying or edginess that's hard to control and shifts easily from one topic to another), *social anxiety* (intense fear about interacting with or performing in front of others, sometimes accompanied by worries about being judged negatively or doing something embarrassing), and *panic attacks* (sudden feelings of terror often accompanied by sweating and heart palpitations).

*Eating disorders.* In a society like ours that places a premium on physical attractiveness, it's not surprising that many young adults are dissatisfied with their bodies and eager to control their weight through dieting or exercise. But when these concerns develop into an abnormal preoccupation with food and weight loss that dominates or interferes with everyday life, it may be time to seek treatment.

There are four major types of disordered eating. *Anorexia* is marked by eating so little that one becomes dangerously thin and fails to recognize that danger. *Bulimia* is characterized by frequent binge eating—consuming large quantities of food in a short period of time—and compensating for this with activities like self-induced vomiting, fasting, or compulsive exercise. *Binge eating disorder* is defined by the same recurrent binge eating as in bulimia, but without the compensatory purging, which often leads to guilt and shame about overeating. *Orthorexia* isn't yet formally classified as an eating disorder, but many practitioners see it as one. It's an obsession with healthy eating so intense that it interferes with normal functioning. People with orthorexia are so preoccupied with what they eat that they may compulsively check nutritional labels and spend a lot of time worrying about what might be served at an upcoming social event. They may stop socializing with others to prevent themselves from eating foods they're not "allowed" to have.

*ADHD.* We all get restless or have trouble concentrating sometimes. But if these times are so frequent that they interfere with day-to-day life or impair one's ability to perform well in school or work, they may be symptoms of adult ADHD. ADHD usually appears during childhood, and it often subsides with age, but many young adults who were diagnosed with ADHD as schoolchildren continue to have the problem. As is the case in childhood, adult ADHD can manifest as a problem of inattention, impulse control, or both. The attentional form shows up as forgetfulness, making careless mistakes, avoiding activities that require prolonged concentration, and being easily distracted. In adults, these symptoms may lead to missed deadlines, disorganization, poor time management, and forgotten plans. The form that's mainly an impulse-control problem, which is far less common among adults than children, is manifested by extreme restlessness or fidgeting, difficulty controlling one's temper, mood swings, and a low tolerance for frustration.

*Substance abuse.* This condition can range in severity from problematic use (using drugs in ways that adversely affect one or more aspects of life), to dependence (needing increasingly amounts of a drug to get the same high, as well as difficulty stopping or cutting back its use), to full-on addiction (needing a drug so intensely that it takes over their life). All drugs have the potential for abuse, including alcohol, nicotine, marijuana, cocaine, methamphetamine, hallucinogens, sedatives, and opioids. Many of these substances are legal for adults to purchase (alcohol, tobacco, and, increasingly, marijuana) and are actively promoted through advertising and marketing, which makes substance abuse especially pernicious because abusing these legal drugs sometimes leads to abusing illegal ones.

Although it's illegal for people under the age of twenty-one to purchase any of these substances, surveys show that most high school students have used alcohol and that nearly half have used marijuana and nicotine (mainly through vaping). Not surprisingly, given that substance use tends to increase over the course of adolescence, many of the same drugs are used by young adults. Other drugs (often referred to as "hard drugs") are illegal for people of any age.

Substance abuse is a problem because of the direct impact of these drugs on the brain, heart, lungs, and other physical systems and because of its impact on the lives of users, people around them, and society. Drug use causes nearly half of all fatal car crashes, contributes to property crime and violent crime (including rape and sexual assault), and is a frequent cause of domestic violence, school failure, lost days of work, unemployment, homelessness, and all sorts of human misery.

Not all people who experiment or even regularly use drugs become abusers or addicts. The problem is that no one knows in advance which users will become abusers and which abusers will become addicts.

❧

Rather than searching for specific symptoms of these disorders in your child, look for more general signs of psychic distress. These include social withdrawal, diminished energy, loss of interest in activities that previously appealed to them, sleep problems (too much or too little), cognitive impairment (memory problems, slow thinking, or difficulties concentrating), unusual eating habits (under- or overeating), restlessness, a failure to keep up responsibilities in school or work, an unkempt appearance, and untruthfulness. Consider whether there have been noticeable changes in any of these realms, especially changes that have persisted for two weeks or more. This will be easier to see if your child is living with you or you see each other frequently, but it's possible to pick up signals in phone conversations or during brief visits, such as secretiveness, frequent lapses in memory, or recurrent problems at work, in relationships, or with the police.

## Getting Help

The earlier a mental health problem is diagnosed and treated, the greater the chances of bringing it under control. This is especially true in young adulthood, when the same neuroplasticity that makes people more vulnerable to the harmful effects of stress also makes them potentially more responsive to therapy.

If you notice a marked change in your young adult's behavior that has lasted for at least two weeks, share your observation with them in a caring, nonjudgmental way ("You seem to be sleeping much more than usual—are you feeling all right?") and ask if there is anything going on. Broach the subject gently and sympathetically, in a way that emphasizes your concern: "You don't seem yourself lately. Do you think it would help to talk to someone about it?" "You've been a little short-tempered the last few weeks. Are things going okay at the office?" "I've heard you up and around during the middle of the night a lot lately. Do you know why you might be having trouble sleeping? When I have insomnia, there's usually something I can't stop worrying about."

※

One of the challenges when you suspect your adult child needs professional attention for a psychological disturbance is persuading them to seek treatment. Many people who have a psychological problem deny or minimize it to others and themselves. Others may not deny the problem, but may be uncomfortable or afraid about addressing it. Our society still stigmatizes mental disorders, and someone who wouldn't hesitate to seek medical care for a twisted ankle or a sore throat may hesitate to see a therapist for anxiety or depression because of concerns over how others, including family members, will react.

As a society we've made many strides on this front, but it's been hard to convince the public that mental health problems aren't moral failings but physical illnesses, just like heart disease, arthritis, or cancer. There are lifestyle changes that can prevent the onset or progression of many illnesses, including many mental disorders, but this doesn't mean that developing the illness was just the result of bad choices. Blaming someone for their eating disorder makes about as much sense as blaming someone for their arthritis.

For others, reluctance to get help is itself a result of the illness. One symptom of depression is loss of motivation—including the motivation necessary to get treatment. Someone suffering from a social anxiety disorder may be apprehensive about talking to a therapist; just the thought of calling to make an appointment is terrifying. Someone whose anorexia has progressed to a dangerous stage may have developed such distorted perceptions of their body that they don't realize anything is wrong, although friends and family can plainly see they're wasting away. Someone with an addiction may have talked themselves into believing that their use isn't a problem, that they can stop whenever they want to, or that they're temporarily overdoing it just to get through a difficult period.

Sometimes people don't want to seek treatment because they're convinced nothing can be done to help them. Your child needs to know that there are effective, scientifically proven treatments for most of the mental health problems common among young adults. Treatment can take time, though, because different treatments are more effective for some people than others (this is often the case with medication). It's not uncommon for a practitioner to experiment with several drugs, either by themselves or in combination, and often along with psychotherapy, before landing on a treatment regimen that works for the patient. If your child insists that "nothing works," reassure them this isn't so, although progress may take time.

Often, a young adult will suffer from a mental health problem they had been treated for previously. If your child responds to your concern by saying that the reappearance of their problem means it's untreatable, explain that some problems that have been successfully treated in the past, like depression or substance abuse, can recur when someone is under stress. Many mental illnesses, like many physical diseases, are chronic. They need to be managed over time, often with the help of medication and regular check-ins with a care provider. It's possible to successfully manage chronic depression, for example, just as it's possible to control a condition like type 2 diabetes or high blood pressure.

Another reason people don't seek treatment is that they know they're ill but their motivation to get better isn't strong enough. For those people, these conditions become habits that are hard to break.

It's probably easiest to comprehend this with respect to substance abuse, because many abusers use drugs for the pleasurable feelings they induce, but other mental disorders, however distressing, can provide a sense of safety or refuge that's comforting in its own way.

My mother was chronically depressed and reluctant to seek treatment. Late one night, when she was about sixty years old, we were discussing it, and she resisted all of my attempts to persuade her to see a psychiatrist to try an antidepressant. Exasperated, I finally said, "Your problem is that you'd rather be depressed than not." She couldn't have agreed more. To her, depression felt like her normal state, its familiarity soothing.

Many people with mental illnesses feel just like my mother did. They can't imagine what it would be like to look forward to things, not worry constantly, not be preoccupied with their weight, or not want to get high. They have long forgotten what it feels like to be happy, tranquil, content, and sober. For them, the fear of the unknown is so powerful that it makes staying ill more attractive than getting better.

⁂

It's especially hard to know when an adult child who hasn't acknowledged that they are having a hard time functioning is showing the signs of a psychological disorder when they live away from home. Even if they're living with you, a problem can be difficult to see if one or both of you is busy with work or other commitments, or if the signs of their illness don't show themselves when they're with you. If they buy their own vodka and drink themselves to sleep every night, you might not notice their drinking problem. If your job requires you to leave the house early in the morning, you may have no idea that they're too depressed most days to get out of bed before noon. If they've been secretly treating back pain with opioids or using a sedative like Xanax or Valium to control anxiety about giving presentations at work, neither you nor they may realize they might be on their way to an addiction.

If you suspect a serious problem, it's important to act quickly. Unless you have training in the diagnosis or treatment of mental health problems, don't try to determine whether your child meets the technical criteria for a disorder before intervening. If it seems that their life is being adversely affected by some sort of mental health problem, that's all that matters. If you were coughing day and night for two weeks, you wouldn't wait to consult a doctor until you had figured out on your own whether you had a cold, bronchitis, an allergy, heart disease, or lung cancer.

Sometimes a mental illness makes a child distance themselves from their parents. Often, their symptoms include pulling away from others—as is the case with depression or substance abuse. This may explain why a child in need of support actively withdraws from those who might provide it. Other young people feel guilty for burdening their parents with something else to worry about; they withdraw from the relationship because they don't want their parents to have to spend time or energy helping them. Still others worry that showing signs of a psychological problem will make them appear more dependent on their parents, a concern that may be amplified in someone struggling to establish their autonomy, as many young adults are. And some may be angry because they believe, rightly or wrongly, that their parents caused or contributed to their suffering. If your child is pulling away for any of these reasons, give them a little emotional room, but make sure they know you're there for them if and when they're ready to reengage with you.

If you bring up your concerns with your child, and they deny them, try focusing on how their behavior affects *you*, not to make them feel guilty, but to communicate your own pain and anguish. "I can't sleep because I worry you might be driving after you've had too much to drink." "You know I'm someone who easily empathizes with others, and when you're anxious, it makes me feel this way, too." "Seeing you so down makes me very sad." "Watching you get so thin scares me." Sometimes, hearing a parent speak from the heart can motivate a child to consider getting help. They may not yet be a parent, but they're old enough to imagine what it must feel like to be this worried about your kid.

There's nothing to stop you from talking with your kid about any struggles you think they're having or offering to help them find treatment. However, there are limits on what you can do beyond discussion because your child isn't a minor. Once they're legally an adult, if they don't want to get help, there's not much you can do unless the situation is an emergency that puts them or someone else in imminent danger (if they're threatening to commit suicide, for instance, or badly injure someone else). In situations this urgent, you should call 911. We live in a world in which firearms and potentially fatal drugs are easy to obtain, and you may not know if your child has access to them. Don't worry about overreacting when their life, or someone else's, may be at stake.

If the circumstances don't require urgent action but you believe your child needs professional attention, you can take one of several approaches. If your child is in school, encourage them to contact their campus's counseling center, which will have a staff of professionals trained in treating young adults. Many university counseling services have been overwhelmed in recent years by dramatic increases in mental disorders among young people, but they maintain waiting lists and have staff who can determine whether someone needs urgent care. If this is the case, they'll arrange for it.

If your child isn't in school and is interested in seeking treatment, suggest they call your family doctor or their own physician and ask for some recommendations. If you have a friend who works in the mental health field, suggest that your child call them for some referrals. It's not a good idea to seek treatment from a friend of the family, however, because of potential conflicts of interest and confidentiality concerns.

You can also help your child research treatment options. There are national hotlines staffed by skilled practitioners for virtually all mental health problems, especially those that often require emergency intervention, such as addiction, anorexia, and suicide—and it's easy to find their numbers on the internet. For less urgent problems, contact information for professional organizations that specialize in specific mental health problems can easily be found online. Representatives from these organizations can identify providers near where your child lives. Make sure you're contacting a professional organization, not responding to an online advertisement for a therapist, practice, or facility.

There's a difference between getting help for your child and helping your child get it for themselves. Unless they're so debilitated that they can't function without your assistance, you want to serve as a source of support and guidance, but let them take the lead. If you called a psychologist and said that your twenty-seven-year-old daughter seems depressed, the psychologist will likely ask a few questions to determine whether she's in any danger of taking her life, and if so, tell you to call 911 right away. However, you won't be able to make an appointment for her without her permission. If the psychologist is qualified to treat the problem you describe, they'll encourage you to have your child call them directly or refer you to another practitioner to pass on to your child. Playing an active role in their own treatment contributes to your child's success.

If you're extremely distressed about your child's situation, you can seek help for yourself, but don't expect that the person you see will also want to take your child on as a patient unless some sort of family therapy is indicated (see "Taking Care of Yourself" on page 71). But even in this case, you can't compel your child to participate.

It's unlikely you'll be personally involved in your kid's therapy, given their age. In rare instances, and with their consent, the therapist may want to meet with you. If your child has entered an inpatient facility, such as an addiction treatment center, your contact with them may be restricted. Don't interpret these limits as a sign that you're the cause of your child's addiction, or that contact with you will imperil the intervention. Many rehabilitation centers create highly structured environments that have proven successful. Maintaining this therapeutic structure may entail strict regulations about visits with family or friends, especially during the immediate weeks or months after entering the facility.

Finally, a word about confidentiality. You care about your child's welfare. You're worried they have a mental health problem that requires professional treatment. You've encouraged them to seek help, and you've helped them find an appropriate practitioner. Perhaps your health insurance is paying for all or part of their treatment. Maybe you've even offered to help pay out of pocket for the portion of the fee that isn't covered by insurance.

Once their treatment begins, though, anything your child discusses with their care provider is strictly between the two of them. Your child may want to discuss their therapy with you, but that's up to them. You shouldn't ask what takes place during their appointments or how the therapy is going. You shouldn't call the therapist to find out how the treatment is progressing (they can't tell you anyway). If your child's therapist believes it would be helpful for you to participate in the therapy, they'll discuss this with your child and encourage them to raise the possibility with you. It's your kid's choice, and no one else's, whether or not to do this.

One important exception to these confidentiality requirements involves college or university counseling centers. In general, these centers are happy to answer parents' questions about things like the availability of services on campus without disclosing specific information about their child. Still, this information may be helpful to parents with children who've recently started college or transferred to a new school if the parents want to let them know where and how to obtain assistance for a variety of concerns. It's best if parents encourage their undergraduate to do their own research by consulting with a resident advisor in their dorm or someone who works at the student health center.

Sometimes students don't know how to research what services are available on campus. Parents can suggest whom to ask about counseling, tutoring, medical care, and the like. Large universities often have complicated bureaucracies, and penetrating them can be overwhelming to an undergrad who's just starting out.

If someone has just enrolled in college and is still a minor, there are some circumstances under which a clinician may want to speak to their parents about difficulties they appear to be having with the transition. This is allowable as long as the student grants permission. A skilled therapist will discuss this with the student and explain why gathering additional information from their parents about things like a medical or family history will be helpful. On the other hand, if you learn your young adult needs counseling (maybe your child's friend has called and told you they're worried about their mental health), you should feel free to call the school's counseling center and alert them. They'll follow up if you ask them to.

Colleges and universities are legally obligated to notify parents if they believe a student is in imminent danger of harming themselves or someone else. In addition, many schools give students the option of signing a release-of-information authorization, which specifies the conditions under which the school may contact the students' parents. It's a good idea to suggest to your child that they do this. Explain that although they are legally adults, they'll still benefit from your involvement and support. Making it easier for the school to reach out to you is better for everyone.

## Taking Care of Yourself

Your child isn't the only one whose mental health should concern you during this time. Many parents of young adults find that the strains of dealing with their kids' issues warrant professional help for them—the parents—as well. These strains range from anxiety to helplessness to depression and beyond.

Susan is one such parent; she watched both of her children's marriages simultaneously fall apart. When he was twenty-seven, her son, Jeremy, had married Beth, a slightly older woman who had a six-year-old son from her previous marriage. Jeremy's parents weren't happy about the marriage. They liked Beth, but thought Jeremy was too young to become a father. Before he and Beth wed, they asked him if he was ready to take on the responsibility—his work as a record producer hadn't really gotten off the ground, and his parents worried that fatherhood would slow his career path even more. Jeremy said he was in love with Beth and was looking forward to raising her son. He had developed a close relationship with the boy while he and Beth were dating.

When Beth's ex-husband found out about the marriage, he set out to make their life miserable. He fought to have their joint custody arrangement revoked and gain sole custody of his son. He harassed Beth repeatedly by phone and would park his Tesla in front of Jeremy's condo and stare at their home for hours at a time. He started to troll Jeremy on social media, attempting to undermine his reputation in the music world.

After enduring the situation for several months—the stress was affecting Jeremy's mental health and his work, and the legal battle was eating into his meager savings—Jeremy decided he couldn't remain married to Beth. Reluctantly, they separated and divorced six months later. The little boy was heartbroken.

"You have nothing to feel guilty about," Jeremy's parents told him when he came over for dinner the night after the divorce was finalized. "That creep was determined to make your life miserable, destroy your marriage, and interfere with your being a good stepfather, and he succeeded," Susan said. "It was an untenable situation that wasn't going to change. Beth knew that—that's what she said. And all the disruption was going to derail your career, which is exactly what he wanted to do." Jeremy excused himself from the table and went into the bathroom.

"It's for the best," Susan told her husband. When Jeremy returned, it was obvious he'd been crying. Though Susan was probably right about the need to end the marriage, it pained her to see her son so devastated.

Little did Susan know that her daughter's marriage was also breaking up. Lily, who was thirty, had been married to Blake for three years when he told her he'd fallen in love with someone else. This was hard enough for Lily to hear, but finding out that Blake had been having an affair with another man for the past year tore her apart.

If her husband had been cheating on her with another woman, Lily would have been willing to go into couples therapy to try to make their marriage work. She had a friend with an unfaithful spouse whose marriage had been saved, even strengthened, through counseling. But Lily couldn't stay married to someone who wasn't physically attracted to her and probably never would be. When she told Blake they had to get a divorce, he agreed.

Lily and Blake had two young daughters, a toddler and an infant. Neither of them had a well-paying job, and they couldn't afford childcare for two kids. They had shared childcare by arranging their work schedules so that one of them was always home. What were they going to do now?

Lily and the girls moved in with her parents for a short time while she looked for a place to live. Her mother watched the girls when Lily went to work, until she and her daughters moved into their own place. Lily hired a full-time babysitter, with her parents' help.

Dealing with both of her children's divorces at the same time took a significant toll on Susan. Both her kids were depressed, and this made her feel the same way. She'd experienced periods of depression previously, and her current stress triggered a new episode. She decided to see her old therapist, who prescribed an antidepressant and weekly counseling. After two months of therapy, Susan decided that the antidepressant was probably enough to manage the problem—she knew from previous bouts what it felt like when the medicine finally kicked in. She stayed on the drug and checked in with her therapist by phone every few months. Her depression subsided after about a year. Soon after that, Jeremy and Lily each remarried, and Susan's life returned to normal, at least for the time being.

Susan knew there was nothing she could have done to prevent Jeremy's or Lily's marital problems. But that didn't make it any easier to deal with them. As the saying goes, a parent is only as happy as their unhappiest child.

If you're going through a difficult time because of problems your child is having and your mental health has been suffering for two weeks or longer, consider discussing the situation with a therapist. If you haven't seen a therapist before, your doctor may be able to recommend someone. Friends and colleagues are also good sources of referrals.

Don't be embarrassed about letting someone know you need to talk to a counselor. Most of us feel overwhelmed by life sometimes, and waiting to seek help may make it more difficult to treat the problem. Psychological problems tend to become harder to treat the longer they're left unaddressed.

If you're struggling with mental health issues due to your relationship with your child, your first step should be to see if the two of you can have an honest and open discussion about the relationship and what each of you can do to improve it. Do your best to hear your child out without being defensive or accusatory, and ask them to do the same when listening to you (see chapter 2, "Resolving Disputes Constructively" on page 40). It may take more than one conversation to reach an understanding and several weeks to get your relationship back on track. It's unrealistic to expect things to change overnight. Hang in there.

If, after several conversations, things don't improve, suggest that the two of you have a few meetings with a therapist. Sometimes, after the first consultation, a family therapist will want to meet with each of you alone to hear both points of view and then start a series of joint sessions in which the two of you explore the roots of your conflict and work to resolve it. Depending on the nature of the problem, the therapist may suggest that you include other members of the family, like your partner or your child's partner.

When asking for a recommendation of a family therapist—from your doctor, a therapist you may have seen in the past, a friend, or a colleague—specify that you'd like to see someone trained in family therapy, because not all therapists are. A good source of information with a directory of family therapists in your area is the website maintained by the American Association for Marriage and Family Therapy (www.aamft.org).

## Estrangement

One of the most dire threats to a parent's mental health is becoming estranged from their child. If you're concerned your differences with your child will lead to estrangement, rest assured that this happens much less often than you may have been led to believe.

If you've scanned the headlines or booksellers' websites, you may think we're in the midst of an estrangement epidemic. But if you read the fine print of the articles or books, or delve into the scientific studies published in reputable journals—as I did while writing this book—you'll come away with a very different take.

Before I looked into this, I thought of "estranged" children as those who had willingly broken off all contact with their parents, and where the breakdown was for some reasonably long period of time. But that's seldom how the term is used. In fact, few writers agree on how to define estrangement. I was surprised by the loose way the term is thrown around and now understand why some media outlets have described the situation as epidemic.

This characterization is misleading. Some studies label parents and children who see each other regularly but have a conflicted or emotionally distant relationship "estranged." Other studies include in their "estranged" group parents and children who haven't seen each other for several months, rather than several years. Some writers describe parents and children as "estranged" if they don't see each other physically, even if they communicate in writing or by phone. I even came across studies in which children reported themselves as estranged from a parent who's long been deceased (and presumably in-communicado). There are studies based entirely on children's reports that label families "estranged" even when the parents didn't know their child felt this way. (Studies that survey parents find rates of es-trangement far lower than those reported in surveys of children.)

Frankly, a lot of the research on estrangement isn't very good and is poorly reported by the media. I found that widely cited re-ports that estimate the prevalence of estrangement at more than one-fourth of adult children grossly overstate the incidence, because this number includes people who are estranged from *anyone* in their family, including siblings and grandparents. When you count only people who are estranged from a parent, the number is well under half of this, and even this number includes people who are in regu-lar contact with their parents but say they don't get along very well. At any given moment in time, plenty of people aren't getting along well with their parents, but I'd hardly describe them as "estranged," at least in the way the term is conventionally used.

I don't mean to diminish the pain of parents who are genuinely estranged from a child, which by all accounts is agonizing. But if you define estranged children as those who, as adults, willingly broke off all contact with their parents for a long period of time—years, rather than months—and you and your child aren't now estranged, your chances of becoming estranged are very small. I can't promise that you won't go through difficult stretches, though.

Who are all these folks the media is referring to when describing estrangement as epidemic?

By far, the largest category—perhaps as much as 80 percent—are children whose biological parents split up, often when the child was young. The child became estranged from the parent who moved out (almost always, their father) because the parent who raised them wanted no contact with the ex.

The adult children give a variety of reasons for this. Some cut off contact with a parent who had been abusive while they were growing up (close to 15 percent of all children in the United States have been maltreated by the time they are eighteen years old). Sometimes they're estranged because the parent with whom the child no longer communicates abandoned the family. In some cases, the mother kicked the father out after his violent, sexually inappropriate or criminal behavior. Sometimes the child's father remarried and began life with a new family that had no emotional room for the estranged child. Yes, technically the child is estranged from their father. But that's probably not what comes to mind when you hear that there's an estrangement epidemic.

The other, far smaller groups usually cut off communication with parents for one of five reasons: (1) the parent refused to accept some aspect of their identity, like their sexual orientation or religious views; (2) there are irreconcilable problems between their partner and their parent; (3) relations between them and their parent had deteriorated over a long time, and they concluded it was better for their mental health to have no communication than to maintain a hopelessly dysfunctional relationship; (4) they won't tolerate one or both of their parents' habitual behavior, like substance abuse; or (5) they and their parent had some sort of intense dispute, perhaps about money, that left them unwilling to continue their relationship.

Tiffany's estrangement was caused by a conflict involving her parents and her new husband, Martin. He and Tiffany had very different backgrounds—her family was well-to-do and his was very poor. They had different education and income levels. But after dating for a long time, they saw how compatible they were and decided to get engaged. But from the moment Tiffany shared the news with her parents, she could see trouble brewing.

When they first learned about the engagement, Tiffany's parents told her it was risky to marry someone who came from such different roots, and that they didn't approve of the marriage. They expected Tiffany to marry someone who had a professional occupation; Martin worked as a laborer for the city's streets department. They expected Tiffany's husband to have at least graduated from college, perhaps gone even further, like their daughter, who had an MBA; Martin had dropped out after the first year of community college. Tiffany's parents assumed her husband would be the breadwinner, successful enough to support her if she chose to take time off from her career to start a family; it was unlikely that Martin would ever earn a tenth of what Tiffany made as a portfolio manager for a hedge fund.

None of this mattered to Tiffany, though. She adored Martin for his kindness, his affection, his goodness, and how much he loved her in return. She was confident he would be a wonderful husband and father, and that, over time, her parents would see this, too.

Rather than asking her parents to pay for a wedding, Tiffany and Martin had a private ceremony at city hall, followed by a quiet dinner with a few friends. When her parents found out, they were livid. They stopped speaking to her.

Months later, Tiffany's parents began calling to see how she was doing. They never asked about Martin, but at least the ice between Tiffany and her parents was broken. Tiffany took this as a sign that maybe her parents had changed their minds, and she tried to organize some casual get-togethers with her parents, her sister, and her sister's husband, figuring that the presence of another couple would ease the situation.

After a year of her parents giving Martin the cold shoulder whenever Tiffany had them over, their relationship with Tiffany began to deteriorate rapidly. They belittled Martin whenever they spoke to her, secretly hoping she would end what they thought was a disastrous marriage. Martin tried his best to be a pleasant son-in-law, but no matter how he behaved, Tiffany's parents refused to welcome him into the family. They adored Tiffany's sister's husband, an orthopedic surgeon whom they always referred to as "the doctor," which only made matters worse.

After these awful gatherings, Tiffany always apologized for her parents' behavior, but Martin assured her that she had nothing to apologize for. He said he'd keep trying to win them over—although she came to realize this was futile. Despite her attempts to maintain a relationship with her parents—including tearful conversations, angry conversations and, ultimately, conversations in which someone threatened to end their relationship—Tiffany decided she had to choose between her husband and her parents. She chose Martin and stopped communicating with her mother and father. It saddened her to think her children would probably never meet their grandparents. She just prayed her parents wouldn't try to stop her sister and brother-in-law from seeing them.

Estrangement between an adult child and a parent can be especially distressing to the family when the child is estranged from one, but not both, parents. It may have been cold comfort for them, but at least Tiffany's parents shared their disdain for her husband and had each other to commiserate with. Imagine, however, if one of Tiffany's parents had been willing to accept Martin into the family, while the other was adamantly opposed to it.

These situations at first appear to hold some promise—perhaps the parent whom the child isn't estranged from can negotiate a tentative settlement between their child and the other parent. If this happens, it's clear a more lasting reconciliation may be possible. But if repeated attempts fail, the parent who's still in touch with the child lands in an impossible situation—caught between their allegiances to their partner and their child. If they end up siding with their kid, it threatens their marriage. If they end up siding with their partner, it jeopardizes their bond with their kid.

I've known families where divided loyalties of this kind persisted for years, with no satisfactory solution. No one caught in this sort of emotional triangle ends up feeling good. Family therapy can help clear the air initially, but if either the child or the estranged parent continues to dig in their heels, there will never be a satisfactory solution, no matter how many sessions they attend. Attempts by the non-estranged parent to negotiate a resolution rarely work for very long, and sooner or later the situation begins to take its toll on both couples' marriages. In most cases I know of, the child ultimately becomes estranged from both parents.

Sometimes an estranged child who has a child of their own uses the grandchild as a means of exerting power over their parents. A parent who attempts to punish or extract favors from their child's grandparents by limiting their contact isn't just hurting the grandparents but harming the child (see chapter 8, "You and Your Grandchild" on page 209). If you find yourself in this situation, it's essential to point this out. You may have a fraught relationship with your child, but if you and your grandchild have been close for years, tensions between you and your estranged child don't have to preclude a warm relationship with your grandchild. You and they both deserve and need that.

❧

Because research on the prevalence and causes of estrangement is so sparse and inconclusive, it's difficult to know what makes reconciliation possible. Repeated attempts by the grieved parent to reach out to the estranged child soon after the child has stopped communicating seldom work. Phone calls go unanswered, letters returned unopened, emails and texts ignored. Estrangement can seldom be remedied easily because it's rarely the result of a single act that might be undone, forgotten, or forgiven. It's exceedingly difficult to heal this sort of rift.

There is good news, though. In many cases, the estrangement just fades after a few years, without any deliberate effort by the parent or the child, sometimes in response to an event that reunites them—like the birth of a grandchild or a serious illness in the family that ignites enough compassion to overcome the alienation. And sometimes estrangement just fades with time. For some adult children, remaining estranged is just too emotionally exhausting.

This is a difficult situation in which patience is a true virtue. Staying in touch periodically, without overdoing it, is probably the best thing the parent can do.

Although full-blown estrangement is rare, almost all parents will go through periods during which they feel distant from their child, because each of them is developing and changing, and change in one person's psychological state often instigates changes in their relationships with others. Your child may be seeing a therapist about marital problems, for instance, and the therapy has led to a revelation about some aspect of their relationship with you. They don't see the need to discuss this with you, but they might not feel like spending a lot of time together until they've fully processed it. Or you may be having a hard time at work and may not feel like socializing with your child—or anyone else, for that matter. It's natural to alternate between periods of equilibrium, when your relationship coasts along on autopilot, and phases when things just don't seem right.

During the trying times, step back and ask yourself what the source of the difficulty is. Sharing your feelings with your partner, a friend, or your child can often be helpful. And, frankly, so can taking a short break from each other. Sometimes a little distance is all you and your child need to ride out a difficult time. If you and they have talked but haven't been able to resolve the tension between you, say something like "I'm glad we've been able to talk about things candidly, but it feels like we're at some sort of impasse. I'm sure we'll get past this, but instead of beating our heads against the wall, let's try spending a little less time together for a while. That's probably all we need to get back to normal."

## CHAPTER FOUR

# Education

## Is College Worth It?

Between the skyrocketing cost of higher education and the oft-told tales of billionaires like Bill Gates and Mark Zuckerberg who made their fortunes without college degrees, it's not surprising that many parents and kids wonder whether college is worth the time and expense.

If you or your adult child is wondering about this, the short answer is "Yes."

For one thing, most of the billionaire dropouts left college to build a business they started while they were students. They didn't drop out until they were already successful. Moreover, these success stories are rare. The vast majority of the world's richest people graduated from college, and half of them also obtained a graduate or professional degree. Believing you can drop out of college and become a billionaire is like hoping to become a starting player in the NBA or a Hollywood legend because you were the star of your high school's basketball team or theater productions.

For those of more modest means, a more practical question to ask when thinking about the value of college is "Compared to what?" If your child doesn't go to college or quits before getting a degree, what will they be doing with their time? Unless they go into one of the skilled trades, like electrician, plumber, carpenter (which increasingly require schooling beyond high school), or certain high-tech occupations, like database administration, people with no more than a high school education usually end up in low-paying positions that don't typically teach the job skills that will be helpful to succeed in a position within the career they hope to pursue, so going to college is probably a better idea than starting a job right out of high school. *Delaying* enrollment is a different question I take up later in this chapter. This is a reasonable alternative to enrolling in college immediately after high school. But the value of doing this depends on what your child does during their "gap year," as I'll explain.

So, here's the bottom line:

From a purely financial perspective, it's certain that college is worth it. This has been studied by economists many times and no carefully done analysis has reached a different conclusion. But to reap the financial benefits, a bachelor's degree is necessary.

If you're sending your child to a four-year college or university, you'd best be confident they'll actually finish with a degree in hand—because about 40 percent of college freshmen never end up graduating. And without a degree, their job prospects are barely better than if they hadn't attended college at all.

Dropping out of college is extremely costly because you and your child will have invested a substantial sum of money in something with very little return. This is especially true for the many students who accumulate a lot of debt and have to pay interest on those loans. So, if you don't think that you and your child have the resources for them to complete a bachelor's degree, it's probably best to wait until your financial situation improves or encourage them to start out at a community college. There, they can accumulate two years of credits they can put toward earning a bachelor's degree at a four-year school. In many states, completing the first two years of school at a community college costs *ten times less* than the first two years in the state university system. Plus, many community colleges have programs designed to help excellent students transfer into a four-year school as a junior. Those that do will advertise this on their website.

College is also "worth it" for many reasons that have nothing to do with economic rewards. Your child will meet people who may become lifelong friends. They may have a professor who sparks a passion for some field they'd never been interested in. They'll discover parts of themselves they never knew existed, things that make them happier about who they are—and perhaps make you happier about who they are, too. If you were lucky enough to graduate from college, think about the things you gained from the experience. I bet there are many items on your list that have nothing to do with how much money you earn.

College isn't only about preparing someone for a job or further schooling. An equally important purpose—maybe even more important—is helping your child develop the self-knowledge, self-reliance, discipline, and maturity that contribute to success in *life*, not just at work. In fact, the "nonacademic skills" college teaches are exactly what employers are looking for—because they help people work well with others, make decisions, find information, communicate fluently both in writing and speaking, think critically, and take responsibility for their work.

## Appropriate Involvement in Your Child's College Education

Several years ago, when I was the director of graduate studies in my university's psychology department, I got a call from a woman with questions about applying to our doctoral program.

"I'm happy to discuss this with you," I said. "Tell me a little bit about yourself and what you're interested in."

"Oh," she replied. "I'm not calling about myself, I'm calling for my daughter."

This was the first time I'd received a call from an applicant's parent in the ten years I directed the graduate program.

"Okay," I said, "just tell your daughter to give me a call, and she and I can discuss her background and what she needs to do to make sure her application is competitive. Many more students apply than we can admit—to be honest, it's a very tough program to get into."

"My daughter's very busy," the mother said, "so I'm taking care of this for her."

I explained that it really was best if I spoke to her daughter directly, because that way I'd be able to fill in important details and answer any questions. I didn't want to have to depend on her mother to be a reliable go-between. It wasn't fair to her daughter.

"You can just tell me," the mother said. "I'll pass the information on to her."

"I'm sorry," I said, "but if your daughter can't find time to do this for herself, I'd worry about whether she's ready for graduate school."

The mother hung up.

I'm glad for her daughter's sake that the mother hadn't mentioned her name. The call would have colored the way I'd read her application—if she (or her mother) ever applied.

I recently emailed a number of colleagues at schools around the country and asked if they had ever had a similar experience. Almost all of them had.

"Are you kidding?" one replied. "I once had a student show up to her interview with her mother, who fully expected to sit in on our meeting!"

❧

I've been interviewing, teaching, and supervising doctoral students for about forty-five years, at three different universities. Phone calls like this one were rare a generation ago. Yet, the students in my seminars haven't changed all that much over the years. They aren't more or less capable, more or less mature, or more or less motivated than grad students were a few decades ago. Their *parents* have changed, though.

I speak for many professors around the country when I say that parents are far too involved in their children's college education, and that this isn't good for their kids' psychological development.

I understand why parents have become so involved, and I don't doubt their motives. But they don't realize how their assistance— whether giving advice about what to major in or what courses to take, editing papers before they're handed in, helping to study for exams, trying to get their child's roommate or room changed, or calling their professors to complain about a grade (yes, all this actually happens)—does more harm than good. I'll explain why shortly.

The increase in parental involvement has occurred for many reasons. First, I think today's parents are more involved in *all* aspects of their kids' lives. As I've noted, they communicate with them far more often than in the past. Second, parents may be more concerned these days about their child's college performance because they're worried about the child's ability to continue their studies or find a good job and earn a living after graduating. Third, parents' involvement in their children's college life is often a continuation of what they did during high school, often inappropriately. And, finally, today's parents are more likely to be "helicopter parents." Some are so hands-on that they've been called "lawn mower parents." They're no longer hovering at one thousand feet; they're down on the ground, clearing a path so their child won't encounter any obstacles.

Since your child's birth, you've had to decide how involved you'd be in various aspects of their life. You've had to balance your wish to help them thrive with the equally important desire that they become independent, competent, and confident. Good parents understand that too much of the first will interfere with the second.

Parents have an especially difficult time striking the right balance regarding their kids' education. They want to make sure their kid is mastering the expected skills, taking the right classes, getting good grades, and doing well on standardized tests.

Most parents understand that as a child progresses from elementary school to middle school and to high school, they should gradually step back and let their child manage more of their own education. Now that your child is in college, your main role is to give them as much financial assistance as you can afford. Forty percent of college students who drop out do so for financial reasons. Leaving college with a bucket of student loans to pay off and no degree only prolongs their financial dependence on you.

*Beyond financial help and a visit to campus once or twice a semester, you should not be involved in your child's college education.*

It's great for you to be *interested* in what your child is doing—what they're reading, discussing in class and with their friends, and discovering about themselves. But don't try to manage their schooling. This may be a radical departure from how you worked with them during their high school years, but now it's time to land the helicopter and put the lawn mower back in the garage.

Unless you're deeply familiar with the particular requirements of your child's major and school, you have no idea how to counsel them about what courses to take and in what order. Degree requirements vary from department to department, and even within a department, from one area of concentration to another. A psychology major who wants to specialize in neuroscience may have an entirely different set of graduation requirements than one who wants to become a therapist.

Degree requirements have gotten so complicated and change so often that most colleges have entire offices devoted solely to helping students figure out what courses they need to take so that they don't discover in April of their senior year that they're missing a course they need in order to graduate that June. It's unlikely that you know enough to provide accurate, up-to-date advice. Your own college experience, thirty or forty years ago, is irrelevant today, at least with respect to graduation requirements.

Nor do you need to do anything to ensure your kid is doing okay in their classes. Their school probably has an extensive network of student services that monitors how well students are doing and provides academic assistance proactively. Course syllabi distributed at the beginning of each semester routinely include information letting students know what services are available on campus and how to access them. Professors receive automated requests throughout the semester to report how every student in each of their classes is doing and alert the university when anyone is struggling so that the appropriate student service office can follow up.

And don't call your child's professors with worries or complaints. If you're ever concerned about your child's academic performance, the best thing to do is to encourage them to seek the appropriate help on campus, because it's surely there. There are even offices dedicated to helping students find services they may not know exist.

In addition to all of this support, colleges provide students with health care and counseling—again, all free of charge. So, rest assured that your child's physical, emotional, and academic well-being are being looked after without you. Their school wants them to succeed, and not only for humanitarian reasons. Dropping out isn't just expensive for students and parents—it's very expensive for schools, too. Schools depend on the income they receive for room and board, and when students drop out, dorm rooms and dining hall seats go unfilled.

And please don't get involved in your child's application to grad school, law school, business school, or med school. It makes you both look bad. More important, you may inadvertently undermine your kid's confidence in their ability to manage their life without your help.

❧

Micromanaging your child's college education will interfere with their psychological growth at a moment when they're primed to acquire the qualities that foster independence. If you can't step back and let them figure out how to manage their life at school, you risk stunting their self-reliance. By doing that you may well hurt their chances for success in the labor force and life in general.

Parents often ask their kids questions like "What are you going to do with a degree in *that* major?" "Why are we spending so much money preparing you for a career in such a low-paying field?" "Why are you taking courses that aren't required for graduation?" These are the wrong questions to ask, and if you're harping on these issues with your kid, you're doing them a disservice.

I've known hundreds of undergraduates who spent the first two years of college majoring in something they hated—and usually did poorly in—because their parents encouraged them to use college as a stepping stone to a high-paying career. I hear more of these stories now than ever. When these students finally get up the courage to face their parents and change majors to a subject they're genuinely interested in, they feel like a tremendous weight has been lifted off their shoulders.

College may be the last time your kid will ever have the opportunity to study something simply because they're interested in it.

That's a graduation gift you can give long before graduation.

## Alternatives to Traditional College

Going directly from high school to college isn't the right decision for a lot of young people. If you're worried your child isn't ready for college or won't get much out of attending, several other options are worth considering.

There are four types of high school seniors who probably should consider doing something other than going to college right after high school.

One group comprises students from families with meager finances. As I explained earlier in this chapter, there's no sense in someone starting college if they won't be able to afford finishing.

A second group are those who can afford it but are academically unprepared for it. About half of entering college students need at least one remedial class, and students who need such classes are more likely to drop out than their peers. Plus, if they're at a four-year school, they're paying a lot to learn things they should have learned in high school, when these classes were (for public school students) free. They'd be better off taking the remedial classes they need at a community college at a far lower cost before enrolling in a four-year program, so that when they're in college they're getting their money's worth.

A third group are those who don't really like school. But some high school seniors who are certain they have no interest in college later become interested in it. For them it makes more sense to delay enrolling than to begin and drop out.

Finally, there are young people who want to take a "gap year." There's no shortage of intriguing, educational ways to spend a gap year. Kids can get an internship in a field that intrigues them, travel, start a business, or volunteer for a cause they're passionate about.

A gap year means you'll probably end up supporting your child for longer than you'd planned. But this might be a wiser investment than paying for college when they're not keen on the prospect. If they're apathetic or bored, they won't learn much or do well, and they may even drop out.

Many parents fear that a student who defers college enrollment may change their mind about going to college altogether, so you should make sure that you and they share an understanding of what this "gap year" is so that your kid makes the most of it. It's time off from school for someone who's sure they want to go to college when the year is over and has formulated a thoughtful plan on how to spend this time. A gap year should not be spent scrolling through TikTok or playing video games.

Colleges often look favorably on students who take a gap year, as long as they've used it productively. It's also possible to apply to a college and request a deferral after getting in. Schools have grown accustomed to this in recent years and have made the deferral process easier. Some schools will grant a request for deferred admission automatically; others will ask to see a plan for how the year will be spent.

For anyone who wants to avoid traditional colleges altogether, the "career college" is a viable alternative. These institutions, formerly known as "trade schools," are designed for those who want training for a specific occupation and don't want to take courses in other subjects, as is usually required to get a degree from a regular college. A career college isn't a good option for kids who are still unsure about what they want to do in life, though, because the education a career college offers is occupation specific. Completing a one-year program of study in culinary arts or criminal justice isn't very helpful if you discover afterward that you want a job in broadcasting.

Many career colleges offer high-quality vocational training, but many others mislead students with false promises that attending their school will guarantee a well-paying job. Stay away from for-profit schools that charge high tuitions, offer little or no financial aid, make exaggerated promises about what their students will be doing after they finish, and aren't accredited by a legitimate professional organization. Some schools claim to be accredited, but their certification comes from a phony or nonexistent organization, so investigate before you put down a deposit. Your state's Department of Education may have resources that will help you figure out if the school is legitimate.

Avoid schools that have a suspiciously high acceptance rate or won't provide information about the proportion of their enrollees who complete the program and their rate of employment in the occupation they trained for. And before you make a commitment, check to see if your local community college offers the same training at a fraction of the cost, which is often the case. Many community colleges have two-year programs designed to prepare their graduates for specific occupations. Some programs place their graduates in apprenticeships, often certified by trade unions, that lead to well-paying, full-time employment.

For young people who want a structured experience that develops discipline and responsibility, joining the military is a good option. Starting salaries are low, but enlistees receive free food, housing, clothing, and health care, plus opportunities to take courses that can be later converted into college credits. After leaving the military, veterans are eligible for benefits that often cover much of the cost of attending traditional college (including tuition, fees, and living expenses), assistance in purchasing a home, free lifetime health care from the Veterans Health Administration, and retirement benefits. Once they've graduated from college, if your kid decides they want a military career, they can apply to Officer Candidate School, which prepares people for well-paying leadership positions. Military recruiters from all service branches are happy to provide information on what is required to receive the complete package of veterans' benefits after leaving.

Many students are already familiar with the most novel alternative to traditional college: online classes. During the pandemic, some found them uninspiring and isolating, but the online experience suits others well for various reasons. Many traditional universities that offer on-campus courses also offer degree programs that run entirely online. Some universities operate exclusively online. Some online courses are scheduled at predetermined times, just like in-person classes, and are often accompanied by opportunities to discuss course material with other students in real time (referred to as "synchronous" courses). Others can be taken anytime ("asynchronous") or a combination of the two ("hybrid").

Online programs have both pros and cons. The advantages mostly involve flexibility. It's possible to pursue studies from any location and to schedule asynchronous classes at times that suit one's lifestyle, which can be handy for those who have jobs. On the other hand, many students lack the discipline to complete coursework on their own and benefit from face-to-face contact with instructors and classmates. Online courses therefore may be more helpful for acquiring specific skills or knowledge than contributing to intellectual and personal development more generally.

As with career colleges, there are both legitimate and untrustworthy online schools, so be sure to carefully research the credentials and reputation of an online program before your child enrolls. Look for online schools that are regionally or nationally accredited and that offer courses whose completion credits can be easily transferred to other institutions, including schools that have actual campuses where they offer conventional classes. Again, check with your state's Department of Education to see if an online program is trustworthy.

All the above options are feasible alternatives to traditional college. The one option I generally would not recommend is your child getting a job right out of high school. There are few well-paying, long-term opportunities anymore for people without a college degree, and most of what's out there are undesirable jobs that don't pay a living wage. If a relative or friend is willing to give your kid a good job, that's fine. But I wouldn't advise your child going out and pounding the pavement with nothing but a high school diploma in hand.

## Visits Home from College

Regardless of whether your child attends a traditional college or follows an alternative path, if they're living away from home, visits home can be tense.

Madison pulled into her parents' driveway after a long drive back from campus and breathed a sigh of relief. She was looking forward to spending spring break at home, enjoying barbecues by the pool, having 24-7 access to an overstocked refrigerator, and sleeping in until the early afternoon. She was also excited to catch up and party with her high school friends, some of whom she hadn't seen in a long time.

A lot of her dorm mates at Emory had driven down from Atlanta and were staying in Daytona Beach, not far from Madison's house. She was excited to mix her college and high school friends and was especially looking forward to introducing her new boyfriend, James, to everyone. He'd be staying with Madison during the last weekend of their break. Being able to sleep together in a full-size double bed was a luxury they eagerly anticipated.

Madison's parents had other plans, though. They hadn't seen their daughter since January. Both her mother and father had arranged their work schedules so that they had more free time during Madison's break. They just assumed she'd spend a fair amount of time with them, playing tennis with her mother, going for the occasional afternoon run with her father, lazing around their pool, and watching movies after dinner with them and her brothers.

She and her mother hugged as soon as Madison walked through the front door, then Madison climbed upstairs to her bedroom, still furnished just as it had been when she lived at home. She plopped her suitcase on the bed, changed into a swimsuit, and went out to the patio, where her father was cleaning the grill. They hugged, and he watched with a smile as his daughter dived into the pool, swam a few laps, climbed onto an inflatable raft, and closed her eyes.

An hour or so later, the whole family gathered around the outdoor dinner table, Madison seated between her parents, holding hands and saying a prayer before they began to eat, which was their custom.

Her father stared at Madison's wrist as he let go of her hand.

"What's that?" he asked.

"It's a tattoo of a little bird. I got it because it's a symbol of being free, of being able to fly away and go wherever you want."

Her father scoffed. "Free, huh?" He refilled his wineglass and was starting to say something about the cost of college when his wife cut him off.

"Oh, before I forget, Maddie, don't make any plans for next Thursday night. We're having some friends over for drinks. They can't wait to see you."

"Um," Madison said, "that's the night James gets here. We won't have seen each other for a week."

"He's welcome to join us, Mads," her father said. "I'm sure everyone would love to meet him."

Madison had made a reservation for herself and James for that very night at a little romantic restaurant in town to celebrate being together again. She was too tired to argue with her parents about the party and decided to bring it up in the morning.

It was downhill from there. Madison's parents refused to reschedule their party, and she had to move her dinner reservation. Her parents complained they never got to see her, what with her sleeping until the early afternoon and her nights out with her friends, some of whom would come back to their house and continue drinking until two or three in the morning. Her friends' loud voices, amped up by the alcohol, woke her parents, which only annoyed them more. A few times, around five in the afternoon, Madison had casually told her parents that she wouldn't be eating at home that night and they shouldn't wait up for her.

By the Wednesday after she arrived, her mother decided they needed to have a talk.

"You come and go as you please," her mother said, "like you're a guest on vacation at your own house."

"Oh, Mother, I'm just not used to having to follow some sort of schedule and report my whereabouts to anyone. It feels weird, like I'm still a child or something."

"Well, you're not living in the dorm this week, and Dad and I would appreciate you showing a little more respect for us and interest in your brothers. You've barely spoken to them all week. It's hardly surprising given how much time you spend sleeping, going out with your friends, texting with everyone, and talking with James."

Madison scowled. *It's supposed to be my vacation*, she thought to herself.

"Speaking of James," her mother said, "I've fixed up the guest room to make it nice and comfy for him."

"Oh, thanks a lot, but you didn't need to do that. We'll be sleeping together in my room."

"No you will not. Not in this house."

"You just said it was my house, too. Anyway, you know we sleep together at school. What's the difference?"

"The difference is that you make your own rules at school, but your father and I make them around here."

Madison didn't argue. She knew that she'd sneak into the guest room or James would sneak into her room after her parents had fallen asleep, and slip back out before her parents got up. She hated sneaking around, but she wasn't going to go yet another week without sleeping with her boyfriend.

College students and their parents often have very different expectations about what visits back home from school will be like. And their different perspectives are perfectly understandable. The student has been living with near complete independence. Some left for school a little nervous about this, especially if they hadn't lived away from home before. But once they'd overcome their initial anxiety about classes, made new friends, discovered they can manage their own affairs, and tasted their newfound independence, it was hard to return to the regimens of the past.

They also have a strong desire, conscious or unconscious, to impress their parents with how mature they've become. It's not uncommon for students to return with new hairstyles, piercings or tattoos, new mannerisms, and newly acquired grown-up habits, like drinking martinis, or new-found preferences for jazz, indie films, or exotic foods. They want their parents to see that the person who left home as a teenager has returned as an adult. And they expect to be treated as one.

Parents are often jarred by the changes. They probably thought something like this might happen—maybe recalling aspects of their own college metamorphosis—but expecting something in the abstract isn't the same as seeing it in the flesh. For their child, becoming an adult is something they've looked forward to for a long time. Many parents, however, have been dreading it.

So it's not surprising that many of the conflicts that erupt during visits home revolve around the student's desire to be treated as an adult and the parents' reluctance, or outright refusal, to do this.

The disagreements usually concern rules that had been in place when the student was still in high school and that the young adult now thinks are absurdly inappropriate—abiding by a curfew; being present for all family dinners (or giving plenty of advance notice); and having to keep parents posted about their activities, schedules, and whereabouts. Parents may feel these rules still apply as long as their child is living under their roof. It's not necessarily an attempt by parents to assert their authority. Their child may be in college, but they still enjoy their company and worry about their safety and well-being. Many parents simply can't fall asleep without knowing that their child has gotten home safely.

And then there are the arguments over things like sex, drinking, and drug use. The student may feel their new status entitles them to do these adult activities openly, as they've been doing at college. Although people under twenty-one aren't legally permitted to purchase alcohol, tobacco, and marijuana, these laws are rarely enforced on college campuses, because it's too hard to prohibit an activity that's illegal for half the student body but legal for the other half, with whom they share housing and social activities. Students aren't asked to show IDs at pregame tailgates or house parties.

Parents don't want to be reminded their child is now an adult, or at least becoming one. It may make them pleased and proud to acknowledge it, but it may also sadden them and make them feel old and irrelevant. They may be fully aware their child is sexually active but don't want to hear that sort of activity in the next bedroom. They may know their child drinks but don't want to see them tipsy. They may suspect their child smokes marijuana but don't want to smell it wafting through the window. To their child, this all may seem hypocritical, but it's perfectly understandable.

Assuming you want your child to keep spending their breaks with you, and assuming they do, too, it's important to figure out how to live together again in harmony. If you approach this challenge with an open mind, some flexibility, and an understanding that these conflicts aren't really about the specific issues, but about the different ways that you and your child feel about their growing up, visits home from college will be much less rocky.

Madison hugged her parents goodbye at the end of the visit and got into her car. As soon as she had backed out of the driveway and headed down the street, everyone breathed a sigh of relief.

"Well, that was just lovely," her mother said sarcastically to her husband as they turned around and walked back into their house.

At the same moment, Madison was on speakerphone with her boyfriend, who had left earlier that morning. "I just escaped from prison," she said, laughing. "Honestly, I think we were all kinda glad it was over."

Neither Madison nor her parents spoke about the visit after she returned to school. But that June, a few days after she arrived home for summer break, her parents said they wanted to talk.

"I think it would help to discuss our expectations for your stay this summer," her mother said. "You know, so that we don't have the misunderstandings we had a couple of months ago."

"Sure," Madison said, "as long as we discuss *my* expectations, too, okay? I mean, I also have some things I'd like to talk about."

"Fine," her father said. "Do you want to go first?"

"Actually, I have a suggestion," Madison said, smiling. "In my business class this semester, we spent a couple of weeks on group decision-making and conflict resolution. One very cool thing we talked about is how to do it collaboratively. The professor divided the class into groups of three and gave us all scenarios to talk through, problems that came from the real world. We had one where a restaurant staff was always arguing about how to divide tips between the waitstaff, the bussers, the hosts, and the bartenders so people got what they thought was their fair share."

She then described an approach much like the one I mentioned earlier in the book, "collaborative problem-solving" (see chapter 2,

"Resolving Disputes Constructively" on page 40). "Our professor said the same technique could be used to settle arguments in families, too. Can we try it?"

Her parents agreed to give it a shot.

"But before we start talking about some specifics," Madison said, "I'd like to say something. I've been doing a lot of thinking about what happened last spring. I think part of the problem is that I've gotten used to being independent, to being an adult. And I think it's hard for you guys to accept that. I'm still your daughter. But I'm not a teenager anymore. And I think this is kind of freaking you out."

"Sounds like you've been learning a few things from your psych class, too," her father said, laughing. "You want us to lie down on the couch?"

"It's not a joke, Dad. And, honestly, what I learned came from talking to my friends, not my psychology class. We're not the only family that's been dealing with this."

After Madison described the process, her father grabbed a notepad and the three of them sat at the kitchen table. Each person mentioned one specific problem—Madison had suggested they start with a limited number of items just to get the hang of it. Her mother wanted to discuss family dinners. Her father mentioned the late-night noisy get-togethers Madison and her friends had. And Madison brought up sleeping with her boyfriend.

They discussed each issue in turn, generating possible solutions and listing them on the notepad. When they had finished, they had four or five possibilities for resolving each dilemma. Then they talked about each potential solution, voicing what they each saw as the pros and cons.

Within about an hour, they had come up with plans they agreed to try. Madison would have dinner with the family every Sunday and at least two other times each week; on days when she had other plans, she'd let her mother know by noon. She agreed to limit the late-night carousing out by the pool to Friday and Saturday nights and to turn the music down by midnight—or to take the party somewhere else, as long as there were drivers who hadn't been drinking or getting high. And her parents said that she and her boyfriend could sleep together in her bedroom as long as they were discreet about it.

When other conflicts arose that summer, Madison and her parents used the same process to generate workable solutions. Over time, as she and her parents came to better understand what they each expected during her visits, their time together became less contentious.

If your child's first few visits home don't go as smoothly as you had hoped, don't assume this will always be the case. And try to use collaborative problem-solving to resolve your disagreements constructively. It will feel artificial at first, but much less so the more often you do it.

Knowing how to resolve conflicts constructively will help a lot. But in addition, as you each become more accustomed to your kid's transition from adolescence into adulthood, they'll feel less of a need to show you how grown up they've become, and you'll become more accepting of their changed, and changing, personality. Most families find that visits home from college become more predictable and less tumultuous each year.

## CHAPTER FIVE

# Finances

## Providing Financial Support

Today's young adults are more likely than those in previous generations to need financial help from their parents after finishing school, largely because the cost of housing has risen far more quickly than salaries, especially in the urban centers that are attractive to people in this age group. And more young adults continue their education beyond college nowadays, which often entails continued financial dependence upon their parents. Increased competition for well-paying entry-level jobs also forces many in their twenties to accept salaries that don't cover their cost of living. Finally, many recent graduates carry large amounts of student debt that must be repaid each month. Given all this, you shouldn't be surprised if your child asks you for financial assistance.

Once your kid's college years are behind them, the topics most likely to stir up tensions between you and them concern money. As I noted in chapter 1, sometime around the age of thirty people's desire to individuate from their parents intensifies again. At this age, being financially dependent on their parents may make them feel they haven't fully arrived at adulthood. And the parents who help their kids out financially would certainly prefer that they didn't have to. But the situation is often unavoidable.

It's crucial to view any request for financial assistance in the context of the prolonged and expensive transition to adulthood that today's young people face. Their trajectory is the norm today. I've said this already, but it bears repeating: You can't judge your child's progress—financially or otherwise—by comparing it to your own experience. When you were your child's age, becoming a self-sufficient adult took a lot less time and money.

Not all parents are in a position to help their child financially, but if you are considering it, there are four main points to keep in mind to avoid any misunderstandings down the road:

- Limit your contribution to an amount that you can handle without worrying about your own finances. Your financial assistance shouldn't jeopardize your health, well-being, or retirement.
- Specify in advance what your help is for and say that you're trusting your child to use the money this way.
- Be clear about how long they can expect your help to last. This can always be revised, but when you offer your help, you should consider how your child's finances may change with time. Someone who needs help while

finishing law school may no longer need it once they're hired by a law firm.

- Let your child know that you expect that they'll inform you when they don't need your help (or as much of it) anymore.

Providing financial support isn't the same as giving financial advice on things like budgeting, spending, and saving. On these matters, wait to be asked for your opinion unless your child is about to do something very unwise with money you've given them. In this case, it's fine to say that how your child wants to use the money you've given them is their choice (see "Purse Strings" on page 110), but that they shouldn't expect you to cover their losses.

Whether and how much you can help obviously depends on your own financial situation. But in addition to deciding how much you can afford to draw from your own income or savings, there are other issues you should consider—whether your assistance is a gift or a loan, how long your support will last, and whether providing help is contingent on how the money will be used. If you have more than one child who needs help, you might reach different conclusions about how much to give or lend each of them depending on their needs. Strive to treat multiple children fairly, but remember that fairly doesn't always mean equally. An elementary school teacher probably needs more help than a corporate consultant.

If you have a partner with whom you share finances, include them in all aspects of the decision-making, whether they're the child's parent or not. Before you present any plan for assistance to your child, make sure you and your partner agree. You don't want to tell your kid one thing only to have to rescind the offer.

It's hard for parents to know whether they should offer assistance without being asked, wait until their child asks for it, or watch for hints that their child needs assistance without them making an explicit request. Some kids might indirectly ask for help by grumbling frequently about the high cost of living or how little their job pays. Be on the lookout for these implied requests.

The main issue isn't who initiates the conversation, but what you say once it begins. Regardless of whether you're offering, your child is asking, or they're dropping hints, this isn't the time for a lecture about fiscal responsibility. That's a fine topic if they ask for your advice at some later point, when they're less likely to interpret what you say as an expression of your opinion about their maturity, competence, or sense of responsibility. For now, the more matter-of-fact you make the discussion, the less likely it is to make your child feel embarrassment, self-doubt, or anxiety about their future.

If you've previously given them money often without waiting for them to ask for it or discussing how they'll use it, and if you're certain they won't feel bad about taking money from you, offer it without any fanfare. It's no different than giving your child any kind of gift. Similarly, if you know your child wouldn't ask unless they needed it, give it without making a big deal about it.

In other circumstances, you should proceed with more caution and sympathetic forethought. Here are some things to ask yourself: Has asking for money always been awkward for your child? Do they seem to have lost some confidence in themselves? Are they struggling financially? If any of these are true, and assuming you can afford to assist them, instead of waiting for your child to ask, take them aside and say, "It looks like money has been a little tight lately. Let's talk about how we can help you out a bit." Use phrasing that indicates you think it's temporary ("lately") and minimize its size ("a bit"); terms like these will soften the blow.

If your child has been dropping hints, and you believe this is their way of asking for your help or feeling you out, it's fine to ask if that's the case. Just make sure not to do this in a way that expresses exasperation ("If you need money, why don't you just come right out and ask us?") or vindication ("Didn't I tell you that you weren't going to be able to afford this place?"), or that will make your child feel dejected or unsuccessful ("I guess it's impossible to live comfortably in this city on what you make"). Instead, show that you understand what they're asking and are fine with the indirect way they're doing it ("Hey, I hear you. Is there anything we can do to help you out?"). This leaves them the option to either say they think they can manage on their own or in fact would be grateful for any assistance. In either case, you'll have eliminated the need for them to ask you directly, which they're probably trying to avoid.

Another way to make the situation less awkward is to offer your assistance as a loan, rather than a gift. This acknowledges that you think the situation is temporary, that your kid is still establishing a career that will offer some financial security down the road, and that you have faith in their responsibility and ability to pay you back. A loan is less likely than a gift to threaten their developing sense of autonomy because it affirms their belief that their economic dependence on you won't last forever.

If you decide to loan your child money, unless it's a very small amount (like a loan at the end of a month for some unanticipated expense), it's wise to put something in writing so everyone is clear about the expectations. If you're thinking about charging your child interest, make sure their payments aren't so burdensome that they'll have to come to you later and ask for a different arrangement. There's no sense in asking a child who's already struggling financially to pay interest on a small loan. This isn't an appropriate forum to teach a life lesson about the costs of borrowing money.

If you're providing financial assistance for an ongoing expense, like rent, you can discuss whether it's better to do this as a lump sum or in regular payments that correspond to the expense your gift is intended to offset, like giving help with rent monthly rather than all at once at the beginning of a lease. If either of you is concerned about your child's ability to stick to a budget, the latter arrangement is better. In either case, though, make sure that you are clear about how long you're expecting to help.

There's one final consideration that's difficult and complicated, and that warrants a separate discussion: whether you have any control over how your assistance is used.

## Purse Strings

Jon and Michelle were looking forward to having their daughter, Vanessa, and her partner, Sofia, spend a long summer weekend with them at their lake house in upstate New York, where the weather would be cooler than in Boston, where Vanessa and Sofia lived. After they finished college, they decided to stay in the area while Vanessa tried to get her baked goods start-up off the ground and Sofia worked for a nonprofit that helped recent immigrants find affordable housing. Vanessa worked on her start-up every weekday night. Most mornings, afternoons, and weekends she worked in the kitchen at one of the city's four-star hotels. Although she was just an assistant pastry chef, she was picking up a lot of valuable knowledge about food preparation as she finalized plans for her own company.

Because the restaurant and nonprofit work didn't pay much, Vanessa had asked her parents if they could help out financially until her company began generating income, which they agreed to do for the few years this would likely take. Jon and Michelle were comfortable financially and happy to help the young couple live in a larger place than they could afford on their salaries so that Vanessa had a kitchen expansive enough to work on product development.

When Jon called to invite them, Sofia picked up the phone. "Any weekend in August that works for the two of you is fine with us," he told her.

"Oh, I'm not sure," she said. "I have to check with Vanessa. We're planning to spend August traveling around Scandinavia. It's the perfect time of year to visit, because the weather is great and it stays light so late. I'll ask Vanessa if we can change our tickets, or maybe we can find a weekend in July to visit, if that's okay with you and Michelle."

"Well, just ask Vanessa to give us a call after she looks into the flights," Jon said.

His wife was reading on the screened porch that overlooked the lake when Jon returned from his call.

"Did you find a weekend?" she asked.

"They can't make it. They're traveling around Scandinavia in August."

"Traveling around Europe? I thought they were broke."

"I guess not," Jon said. "Either that, or we're treating them to a vacation. It must be nice to jaunt around Copenhagen and Stockholm on your parents' dime. Scandinavia isn't exactly cheap."

"Maybe Vanessa is hoping to get some product ideas over there," his wife said.

"Expensive cookies," Jon muttered as he headed back into the house.

One of the most difficult questions a parent faces when they're subsidizing their adult child's income is whether they should have any say in how that subsidy is used. This is a particularly sticky issue when a parent's contribution goes toward ongoing monthly expenses, like rent or preschool, rather than a one-time outlay, like an auto repair or dental bill, or a special purchase that they're happy to view as their treat, like a new television or mattress. When your help is ongoing, there's no way to verify exactly how it's being used.

You could designate your assistance for a specific purpose, like housing, but these designations are impossible to enforce. Vanessa's parents provided financial assistance to help with the rent—that's what Vanessa had asked for. If her parents were to complain that the money was being used to pay for a vacation, Vanessa and Sofia could easily (and honestly) say that it wasn't—that they'd saved enough for the trip by cutting back on other expenses, like groceries or clothing, and Vanessa's parents would have no way of knowing.

Before offering financial help, think about how you'll feel if your child proves to be more of a spendthrift than you'd realized and whether or how you'd voice your concerns. If the help was offered with no strings attached, don't say anything if their spending bothers you, even if you presumed it would be put toward basic living expenses. But if your child asked for help making ends meet, and their version of "making ends meet" includes a lot of extravagances, it's fine to ask about it. You can say something like "I'm wondering whether you still need our help, or need as much as we've been giving you—it seems like you're doing just fine," without mentioning the specific expenditures that concern you.

There's nothing wrong with parents indicating how they would like their monetary support to be spent, and some parents specify in advance that their assistance is for particular items, like housing, childcare, or education. Whether this is how the money is actually used is a matter of bookkeeping, though, and when your child says they need help because their rent has gone up, their day care provider has increased their fee, or they'd like to go back to school, you simply have to trust that they're being honest.

If you think their spending is too lavish and you can genuinely use the money you're giving them for something you need, like a long-awaited home improvement, it's fair to say something like "I'm wondering whether you still need our help—from the looks of it, it doesn't seem as if you're having trouble making ends meet, and we could really use the money to renovate the kitchen." Phrase this in a general way rather than grilling your child about a specific expenditure that bothers you or asking to see their monthly budget. Just because you're helping your child financially doesn't mean they can't have the occasional dinner out or otherwise splurge once in a while without your approval.

This is how Michelle suggested that she and Jon look at Vanessa and Sofia's trip to Europe.

"The trip may seem like an extravagance," she told him, "but they both work very hard, and I don't think we should begrudge them the only vacation they've taken in the past two years. Besides, we don't know whether they scrimped on something to save up for the trip. If they cut back on weekly groceries and put the savings aside to pay for their plane tickets, would you feel different about it? Or do you think that every time they save a dollar here or there they should return that much of our rent subsidy?"

"No, I see your point," Jon said. "But suppose we needed the money for something? Would we have the right to say something then?"

"Well," Michelle said, "if we really needed the money, we shouldn't have offered to help in the first place. And fortunately, we don't. But if something unexpected came up—say we discovered the roof on this cabin needed to be replaced—I think we could tell them we have to reduce what we've been giving them. I'm not sure what they'd do to make ends meet, but I'm sure they'd understand. And I'd want to tell them far enough in advance so they'd have time to make a plan."

As it turned out, Vanessa and Sofia had worried about how Vanessa's parents would react to the news of their trip, and when Vanessa called back later to discuss a date for their visit to the lake, she brought it up.

"Before we decide on a date, I wanted to explain where we got the money for our trip," she told her father.

"You don't owe us an explanation," he said.

"I know we don't, Dad," Vanessa said, "but Fia and I talked about it, and we thought we should say something. We didn't want you to think we were spending your rent money on an expensive vacation. Fia's mom gave us the plane tickets as birthday presents, and we put ourselves on a budget and stopped buying things we didn't really need to save money for hotels and meals. You'd be amazed at how all those lattes add up when you stop by Starbucks twice a day."

"That was very sweet of Sofia's mother to do that."

"Oh, gosh, Dad. We are so lucky to have parents who are so generous. Honestly, I don't know what we'd do without you."

## Helping with a Home Purchase

No financial transaction between parents and children has more potential to strain their relationship than helping with their first home purchase. Helping your kid buy a home has both financial and psychological ramifications, and the latter are often more challenging than the former.

The financial parts include giving or loaning money for a down payment and helping calculate what they can afford—and what they might need—each month on loan payments, property taxes, insurance, utilities, and so forth. Offer to answer any questions about different mortgage options, computing closing costs, and suggesting strategies for submitting offers and counteroffers. Because this is your child's first home, they may have only a cursory understanding of these matters. This is a situation with a lot of detailed information to sort through, and a second pair of eyes may catch things that the first pair missed. This is the perfect way to explain why you're proposing to help in case you're nervous about how your offer will be received.

Other players, like realtors, mortgage brokers, and lenders, will offer your child advice about these matters, but they have vested interests that may not align with your child's. As someone who may be more experienced and wiser than your kid—and who can distance themselves emotionally in a way that's hard for an eager first-time home buyer—you can protect them from being taken advantage of.

※

Providing help with the down payment is straightforward. Take stock of your own finances and, if you're so inclined, give or lend an amount you can afford. Tell your child in advance the maximum you can provide so they can keep this in mind when they start considering properties. If you are thinking about cosigning a mortgage loan for your child, be careful; keep in mind that you will have to take over or contribute to the payments if your child isn't able to make them.

If it's a sellers' market and customary for houses to go for more than the asking price after a bidding war, take this into account when deciding how much help to give. You might say, "We're planning on giving you this amount toward the down payment, and, if necessary, we'd be able to find this much more if you have to increase your initial offer, but that's as high as we can go." This way, your child can compete with other potential buyers knowing their limit.

Depending on the amount they're planning to provide, many parents find it makes more sense to structure their help as a loan rather than a gift. This is something you'll want to discuss with a tax expert. There's a legal limit on what a parent can "gift" to a child without it affecting the taxes on a later transfer of assets. As long as you stay within this limit, you may also gift money to your child's spouse without worrying about the tax consequences. If you're married, you and your spouse can each gift money to your child and your child's spouse, so the combined amount you and your partner can give the house-buying couple is four times what either of you can give your child alone.

There are no restrictions on how much you can *lend* your child, though. If you're going to loan them a substantial amount for the down payment, consult with an expert before you make any concrete plans. There are legal requirements about the size, term length, and interest rate charged on "family loans." For family loans above a certain amount, the IRS *requires* that you charge your child interest, but lets you set an interest rate significantly lower than what banks are charging at the time on similar loans. Different rates are specified by the IRS for loans of different lengths; this information is available on its website. Once you've settled on the specifics, document them in writing, and make sure you and your child keep these records, because they may be necessary for tax purposes.

If you can lend your child a large amount of money, your loan might be enough to help beyond a down payment and replace or supplement a mortgage. This will save your child a lot of money, because the interest rate on a family loan can be quite a bit lower—sometimes by half—than on a loan from a commercial bank or mortgage company. Additionally, your loan will generate income for you each month from the interest your child pays you—most likely considerably more than if you had left the money in a savings account. In other words, by setting up a family loan, your child might end up paying half as much in interest, and you might earn twice as much in interest, as each of you would if the mortgage were provided by a bank or other lender and you kept your money in a savings account. If your child wants to deduct the interest they pay you on their taxes, talk to an expert about how to document the loan as a mortgage.

Ken and Amanda were in a position to help their daughter, Annie, and her husband, Douglas, in this way. Annie and Douglas, who worked in Kansas City, had a child preschool-age and another on the way. During the pandemic, when they were forced to work from home—Annie on her laptop at the kitchen table and Douglas in their bedroom—they realized they would soon outgrow their two-bedroom apartment if they were going to keep working remotely, as they expected they would. They began looking for a place in the suburbs large enough to raise a family, use a room for a home office, and have a yard. The couple had saved $100,000 for a down payment and were planning on getting a mortgage for the balance. They found a house they liked for $400,000. At the time, mortgage rates were around 5 percent for an interest-only loan.

Annie's parents planned on helping the couple out with a gift of $50,000. But once they learned about family loans, they thought about supplementing their gift with one. At the time, they had the bulk of their savings in a bank account that was only earning 1 percent in interest, and they had no immediate plans for the money. (It is possible, of course, that interest rates on your savings account will increase over time; I'm using this figure only to illustrate how the process works. And keep in mind that if you need to sell off investments to fund the loan, you may have to pay taxes on any income your investments had generated.)

Because the IRS rate for long-term family loans at the time was 3 percent, Annie's parents offered to loan her and her husband an additional $250,000 at 3 percent, considerably lower than what Annie and Douglas would pay on a mortgage from a bank. They agreed that Annie and Douglas would repay the $250,000 loan when they sold their house. Annie and Douglas would make monthly payments of $625 to her parents for as long as they owned the house rather than the $1,042 per month in interest they would pay on a mortgage, saving the couple about $5,000 per year. And Annie's parents, rather than earning $2,500 per year in interest from their bank (1 percent on $250,000), would receive $7,500 per year in interest from Annie and Douglas. They put the terms in writing and signed.

❧

Regarding other issues that arise when one is buying a home—like what your child can afford to spend, different mortgage options, closing costs, and strategies for negotiating the purchase details— your primary role should be asking questions to make sure your child hasn't overlooked anything. It's easy for someone who's never owned a house to forget things like insurance premiums or home-owners association fees.

The same is true for closing costs. A lender will provide the specific details at a later point, but your child might not think about them before starting to shop, and on an expensive home purchase, these costs can be surprisingly high. Sometimes the up-front costs of the purchase put a house out of reach for couples on a tight budget.

I'm not suggesting you do the math on all of these matters, just the reminding. You'll save your child time they might otherwise waste looking at properties they can't afford. Once they're ready to make an offer, ask them if they'd like any advice before starting any negotiations. If they turn you down, don't pursue it.

Deciding about your potential involvement in the *nonfinancial* aspects of purchasing a home, like evaluating a neighborhood, identifying strengths and weaknesses of specific houses, thinking through what might need to be done to make a house livable or improve it in the future, and making a final decision about whether to make an offer, is a lot trickier than financing a purchase. Your child probably wants your help with the money. They may have very different feelings about hearing your opinions about which house to buy, though.

Your involvement in the financing should have nothing to do with your involvement in the selection of a house, and you need to unlink the two. Helping to fund the purchase doesn't give you the right to dictate how the money is spent, nor does it give you any veto power over a final decision. The size of your contribution doesn't matter.

If you're unwilling to help with a down payment without having a say in the final decision, you either need to rethink whether you want to provide assistance or make it clear when you offer it that having a say in the decision is part of the deal. Whatever you decide, don't withdraw your offer of help after your child has announced their choice because you think they're making a mistake. Unless you're going to co-own the property, you're their benefactor, not their business partner.

As for scouting houses that are on the market and in your child's price range, you should ask if they'd like your help. Some young adults are so busy with work or parenting that they welcome anyone's help. Others would rather look on their own because they enjoy making their own discoveries and finding bargains, or simply because they enjoy looking at real estate listings. If you hear of a new listing before it's been publicized or know about a house that's about to be put up for sale, it's fine to pass this information on.

Because so much real estate information is online, it's easy for your child to send you links to listings of interest. If they do, resist offering your opinion unless they ask for it. They may just be excited to show you what's for sale in a neighborhood they're considering or show you their dream house, even if it's priced well above what they can afford. Similarly, if you'd like to accompany them when they tour a house, wait to be invited, but take them up on the invitation if you can. Some couples may want to see a property on their own first before returning with a parent, if only to screen the house before asking someone else to look at it.

None of this means you can't express any opinions during the search process, or that help with a down payment is a prerequisite for speaking your mind. I know I've said all along that the basic rule of thumb is to speak your mind only when it's necessary to prevent a potential disaster, but you can relax this principle when it comes to buying a house. Relative to their income, it's likely the largest investment your child will ever make.

If your kid tells you to keep your opinion to yourself, you should respect that. But point out that they're making a momentous decision that has important implications, some of which can't be changed unless they sell the house—like where their child will be going to school or whether they'll be so house poor that they'll be stressed out and miserable. Your input may be especially valuable if you've purchased or sold one or more homes of your own.

Assuming your child doesn't explicitly ask you to stay out of it, the key isn't whether you express your opinion, but how. The best way to do this is by asking pointed questions and framing them in a way that gives your child pause but that allows them to disagree. "The layout looks great, but are you worried about whether the main bedroom is big enough for your queen bed? Do you think you should go back with a tape measure?" "The brochure emphasizes brand-new kitchen appliances, but from the diagram the realtor gave you, it looks like there's almost a complete lack of counter space. That will be hard to live with for someone who cooks as often as you. Are you willing to remodel the room?" "There are a lot of restaurants and clubs nearby. Do you think you should come back on a weekend night and see whether it's noisy?"

Because choosing a first home is often driven by strong emotional responses, it's easy for an inexperienced buyer to zero in on a single feature that's especially attractive at first sight—a screened porch, a stained glass window, a funky entryway, a professional stove—and not pay enough attention to things that are less fun but more fundamental. A screened porch may be irresistible, but if your child buys a house that has major plumbing problems, outdated wiring, a crumbling foundation, or a leaky roof, they're going to be spending more time (and plenty of money) fixing these essentials than enjoying iced tea and summer breezes on the porch. If you see potential problems but your child is resistant to hearing about them, suggest hiring an independent expert to provide an unbiased opinion. By the same token, inexperienced buyers may be too quickly put off by flaws you know are easily remedied. Many new home buyers are thrilled to learn that shortcomings they see in a house they love are not hard or expensive to correct.

This is why you can take a more active role in helping your child purchase their first home than you might in other situations. You shield them from being swindled, while protecting them from making an impulsive or shortsighted decision to purchase or pass on a house.

## Discussing Your Personal Finances

Every parent won't need or want to help their child buy a home, but all parents should discuss their own financial future with their child. If you haven't yet done so, one frequently recommended guideline is to follow the "40-70" rule: Have the conversation before your child reaches forty and before you turn seventy. There's no reason you can't begin some aspects of the discussion earlier, when your child is in their twenties, but you should probably wait until you can reliably forecast your own later financial needs before digging deeply into the topic with them.

Because there may be a lot of ground to cover, discussing your finances with your child is best done in multiple conversations that are short enough to maintain everyone's attention and allow for questions. Your first one should be very general. Its purpose is to let your child know three things: whether you'll have enough money after you retire to live comfortably, whether you'll need some sort of assistance from them, and whether they might inherit anything from you. This conversation is better done in person, but if that isn't possible, you can do it by phone or videoconference. Don't handle this by text or email, though, because those mediums are more restrictive and less informative than a frank conversation.

If your child wants to have their partner present, that's okay, as long as you're comfortable with it. If you have more than one child, you can meet with them separately or jointly, whichever is most convenient. As I'll explain, this first conversation is one in which you should avoid sensitive issues, like actual dollar amounts and who might inherit what, so you can avoid strong emotions or outright conflicts.

Whether your partner is present for this initial discussion is up to you and them to decide. Either way, the two of you should talk about your joint plans thoroughly beforehand and make sure you agree about what to convey when you sit down with your kid. If you and your partner don't agree on certain details, sort them out before you talk to your child. If you're going to handle this discussion on your own, make clear to your child at the outset that you and your partner have agreed on all the details you'll be sharing.

Generally, I've advised waiting till your kid asks you questions or seeks help, but here it's essential that you make the first move. They need to know about your retirement plans, your long-term financial health, and related matters, but they may well be reluctant to ask you directly. Such questions are delicate by nature, and many kids don't want to ask because those questions remind them that you're getting older—a prospect that makes many kids uncomfortable, even anxious. Your child may have questions or worries about how you and your partner will fare after you stop working. They may wonder whether you have enough insurance for medical expenses and long-term care, since these are two categories of expense that, if left uninsured, can impact an entire family, including them.

Retiring may seem far off to someone who isn't yet forty, but if you've spent a lot of time thinking about and preparing for your post-employment life, you have a lot of knowledge to share with your child, and you might not be around when they're approaching their own retirement. It's good for them to see how you're thinking about these things. And if they haven't yet thought about planning for their own financial future, tell them they should. It's well established that to live comfortably after you retire, you have to start saving soon after you begin working.

You'll also want to prepare your child for decisions they may have to make if you or your partner becomes ill or otherwise unable to manage your finances. There's a good chance one or more of your kids will have to be involved in this at some point, and it's important for them to know what you'd like them to do if the necessity arises. If you have a plan, you want your child to know what it is and how to put it into place. If you're already suffering from a serious illness that at some point may leave you incapacitated, don't wait until you turn seventy. They need some basic information about your financial affairs before there's an emergency they have to handle. At a minimum, this includes contact information for any accountants, attorneys, or financial advisors as well as copies of your will, living will, and powers of attorney.

Your child should also have your financial account numbers and information on how to access them. Make a record for your child, but keep the account numbers, log-in IDs, and passwords in separate documents or electronic files. Tell them where to find hard copies of various financial and tax records and how to access important information on your computer, and get in the habit of updating this information periodically and keeping your child up-to-date. If something happens to you that requires your child's involvement in your finances, like paying bills if you're too ill to do so yourself, you want to make it as easy as possible for them. Prepare a document with instructions on whom to pay each month, from what account, and through what mechanism (check, credit card, electronic transfer, etc.), and tell your child where to find it. It's especially important to do this if your partner hasn't been involved in these matters, so that your child can help them if necessary.

※

When you first broach the subject of your financial future, your child may wonder whether they'll inherit anything from you, and, if so, what their inheritance will be. If it's the first time they've asked about it, you should answer this question honestly, but in general terms ("I think so," "Probably not," or "I don't know yet"). Tell your child you'd like to have a separate conversation about the specifics after you've come up with a plan. You may be reluctant to talk about this, but it's essential your child knows what they can expect when you pass on, so they can make short- and long-term plans that take into account what they may, or may not, inherit, including valuables and real estate as well as money. If you have more than one child, all of them need to know what they can expect to inherit.

We've all seen movies and TV shows about conflicts that erupt within ultra-wealthy families over inheritance, but discussing inheritances in detail can raise sensitive and emotional issues regardless of how wealthy you are, especially if you have multiple heirs. Even families who don't have a lot of money to pass on often have prized possessions that have financial or sentimental value, like jewelry or heirlooms. You may have to decide what your plans are for your house—whether to pass it on to one or more heirs or sell it and divide up the profits. You don't need to own a mansion to worry about how your child will feel about your plans to sell a house they're attached to.

If you haven't yet given it a lot of thought, now is a good time to make some preliminary decisions about how you will divide up any assets you plan on passing on to your child and any other potential beneficiaries. You may already have a will drawn up, but if it was written many years ago, it may need to be updated to take into account any changes in your family life or your estate since the will was last revised. If you have a sizable or complicated estate, you should seek the advice of one or more experts.

Once you've made up your mind, it's best to discuss the inheritance with your family in two installments: one in which you describe a preliminary plan and explain the reasoning behind it, and a second in which you present a final plan after you've had a chance to think about any fresh issues that arose during the first conversation. You may learn during the first conversation that your child cares less about certain valuables than you had assumed, or that they and their siblings have already had their own talk about the inheritance and have come to an agreement about how various components of your estate should be divided among them. There's no point in obsessing about which child should inherit a piece of real estate when they and their siblings have already agreed to sell the property and divide the proceeds equally.

The first conversation is your chance to explain why you left certain things to specific people or designated them to play key roles in administering your will. Potentially charged topics include how you plan to divide your assets among different family members; whether you're leaving anything to charity or people other than family members; and how the inheritance will be handled if you die before your partner, especially if they're not your child's other parent. Many financial planners suggest you have a financial advisor or attorney present to answer technical questions and create a professional atmosphere that will minimize fraught reactions and interactions. They can also serve as mediators to help resolve disputes between family members, should any surface.

There is no way to avoid feelings of disappointment, resentment, or anger when a child thinks they're being treated unfairly. Discovering that their inheritance will be much smaller than they'd anticipated, that you aren't dividing the inheritance evenly among siblings, or that a stepparent will be inheriting a substantial portion of your estate may elicit strong emotions. That's a good reason to handle these topics with extra care, perhaps even beginning this part of the conversation with something like "Some of our plans may surprise you, but let's talk about them so that you understand our thinking. And please ask any questions you might have." A disappointed child may feel less angry once they've heard your reasoning.

The final decisions are for you and your partner to make, but letting any intended beneficiaries ask questions and hear your reasoning will minimize conflict and misunderstanding.

In addition to explaining how you wish to divide your estate, you should discuss what roles any of your children may play, including who, if any, will have your powers of attorney for health and finances and who will serve as executors of your estate. Even if you designate your partner for these responsibilities, you'll have to decide which, if any, of your children will be next in line or expected to share some of them. Make these decisions based on your children's skills and abilities. One of your kids may have an expertise in medicine or finance; another may be more organized and detail-oriented.

If you have more than one child, dividing your wealth equally among them may seem like the fair thing to do and a good way to avoid conflict between siblings, which is why the majority of parents follow this strategy. But sometimes it's more important to give the most help to those who need it most. If one of your kids has a child with health problems that will generate considerable medical expenses, for example, it makes sense to take this into account. Leaving a valuable heirloom to a child who has always admired it makes more sense than flipping a coin and passing it on to whoever wins the toss. When deciding how to allocate your estate, remember that fairness does not always mean an even division of assets. It's fine to treat your kids in different ways depending on their individual needs. Just make sure your decision makes sense and that they know your reasoning. You may be pleasantly surprised by how understanding they are.

❧

In the financial realm, your kid will need to acclimate to your needs, preferences, and goals. In the romantic arena, something like the opposite should happen: you'll need to take into account *their* needs, preferences, and goals. That's the focus of the next chapter, as we look at the typical progression of romantic life during early adulthood, from sexual activity to the selection of a long-term romantic partner, the wedding (or comparable celebration), changes in your relationship with your child after they've gotten married, establishing a bond with your child's partner, and dealing with the new couple's marital conflict if and when it occurs, even if it progresses to separation or divorce.

## CHAPTER SIX

# Romance and Marriage

## Your Child's Sexuality

Few aspects of life are more personal than someone's sex life, sexual orientation, and gender identity. Whether your child chooses to reveal or discuss aspects of their sexuality with you is entirely up to them, just as whether you decide to share information about yours is totally up to you. Families differ in how comfortably and casually they talk about sex, and there's no single right way to think or feel about this topic.

For the most part, you should stay out of your child's sex life unless they approach you to ask or reveal something, or unless you're certain they're behaving in a potentially dangerous way, like unprotected sex with strangers. And if your child lives with you, you should certainly not snoop around trying to learn things about their intimate relationships they'd probably prefer to keep private.

Depending on how close you and your child are, the two of you may feel comfortable talking about sensitive matters such as their worries about the quality of their sex life, sexual problems they're experiencing with their current lover, or an unintended pregnancy they aren't sure what to do about. You should listen patiently, resist giving advice unless you're asked for it, and keep the conversation confidential. If you'd like to get your partner's opinion on something you and your child have talked about, ask your child for permission.

If you learn your child has been the victim of any sort of abuse, harassment, or inappropriate sexual behavior, ask if they would like to talk about it with you. If they do, listen sympathetically, assure them that they're not responsible for what happened, and encourage them to make a report to someone in a position to do something about it. As we've learned during the last decade, sexual victimization is far more common than previously thought, and policies have been implemented in the workplace and at colleges to prevent and respond to it. If the incident has affected your child psychologically, suggest they speak with a counselor. And if something of this sort happened to you when you were younger, consider telling your child about it and how it made you feel. It will help them to know they're not alone.

Learning about their kid's sexual history, whether it includes victimization or not, makes many parents uncomfortable. The same can be true about the fact that your child is sexually active, a reality that many parents have had to confront as more and more adult children have moved back home. (For purposes of this discussion, I'm

assuming that the young adult isn't married. Whether you are mor-
ally opposed to sex outside of marriage isn't the issue; presumably,
you feel this way regardless of where the sex is taking place. By the
same token, if a married child and their spouse have moved in with
you, the fact that they are sexually active shouldn't be a concern.)

If your child has been living away from home and has enjoyed
an active sex life, it makes sense that they'd like to continue this activity. But if you're like many parents, you're comfortable knowing
your kid is having sex as long as the activity is taking place somewhere other than your home. Perhaps you feel this way. You can't
put your finger on the reason, and you know it doesn't make any
sense, but you'd just like to have more distance between yourself
and your child's sex life.

There's a good explanation for this feeling: we don't like thinking about our children as sexual beings, which is why we can tolerate
our children having sex someplace where we don't have to face it,
but not when it's right down the hall. If it's any consolation, your
kid would probably like to keep their sex life as far away from you
as possible.

This is a challenging situation that cries out for patience and
mutual respect. It may help to know that people are more sexually
active during their twenties and thirties than at any other age, so the
fact that your kid wants to have a sex life is natural. It's unreasonable
to expect a grown child who has no choice but to live at home to be
abstinent just because their sexuality is too hard for you to handle at
close range.

If the problem isn't that your kid is sexually active but that you
don't want to have to be reminded of it, there are steps you and they
can take that will make things easier. The solution isn't to insist on
abstinence, but to expect that they will do what they can to keep
their sex life private—but private doesn't mean secret. There's no

reason to prohibit an adult in their twenties or thirties from being sexually active under the same roof as you, as long as everyone is respectful of each other's privacy.

You shouldn't force your child to sneak around, but you should insist that they be discreet. If you believe they're carrying on in a way that's indelicate or offensive, speak up. It's okay to say something like "Your sex life is your own business, but this is a small house, and the walls are thinner than you think. Please try to be a little more discreet. Or feel free to sleep at their place."

❧

Young adulthood is also when children often tell their parents about their sexual orientation or gender identity. Many people confuse the two. *Sexual orientation* refers to someone's enduring pattern of emotional, romantic, or sexual attraction to others (e.g., gay, straight, bisexual, etc.), whereas *gender identity* refers to someone's internal sense of their own gender (i.e., male, female, both, or neither), which may or may not be the same as the sex they were assigned at birth. Transgender people are those whose gender identity differs from the sex they were assigned at birth, usually on the basis of their genitals. "Cisgender" describes people whose gender identity remains consistent with their assigned sex at birth.

Someone's sexual orientation has nothing to do with their gender identity—someone who identifies as male can be straight, gay, lesbian, bisexual, or asexual, as can someone who identifies as female, a combination of male and female, or neither. Moreover, someone's sexual orientation and gender identity don't necessarily correspond to the way they express their gender—whether they behave in stereotypically masculine ways, feminine ways, or a mixture of each. You can't tell someone's sexual orientation or gender identity by their physical appearance or their behavior. Portrayals of effeminate gay men or hypermasculine lesbians in popular media are nothing more than stereotypes.

Neither sexual orientation nor gender identity is a choice. You can't change someone's sexual orientation or gender identity any more than you can change their height. Attempts to "convert" someone's sexual orientation or gender identity are not only unethical, cruel, and ineffective, they have harmful psychological effects, including depression, anxiety, and suicidality. Similarly, efforts to discover the root cause or reason for someone's sexual orientation or gender identity are pointless, because like most aspects of who we are, our sexuality is influenced by a complex mix of genetic, hormonal, and environmental factors, some of which are present before birth. We never ask why someone is straight. There's no reason to ask why someone is gay, either. A sexual orientation other than straight, or a gender identity other than the sex assigned at birth, isn't an illness, disability, or problem. Problems only arise when other people fail to accept someone's sexual orientation or gender identity.

Although society's tolerance for diversity in sexuality has increased, many people whose sexual orientation or gender identity is "nonconforming" (that is, different from the prevailing expectation that people are straight and identify as the gender they were assigned at birth) still encounter intolerance in their families, schools, workplaces, and communities, and this intolerance frequently leads to mental health problems. Parents' refusal or reluctance to accept their child's sexuality is especially devastating, and it sometimes causes irreparable estrangement between a child and their parents (see chapter 3, "Estrangement" on page 75).

Finally, someone's nonconforming sexual orientation or gender identity doesn't mean that they can't marry or become parents.

Today, same-sex couples marry, adopt children, and have babies with the assistance of a surrogate mother or in vitro fertilization (IVF). There is no need for parents to worry that having a gay or lesbian child means they won't be able to enjoy the pleasures of grandparenthood. The same is true for parents of transgender children.

Parents vary in how they feel when their child reveals a non-conforming sexual orientation or gender identity to them. Some parents believe they've known this about their child for some time and are relieved their child feels secure enough to tell them. Others are surprised by the revelation, but also are glad their child has been open and honest about this aspect of their life. Some are quietly unhappy and tell themselves this is a phase that will pass. Others are distressed, wish their child's revelation wasn't true, and say as much.

A child who has waited until young adulthood to reveal their sexuality to their parents has likely been holding off doing so for years, because most people come to understand their own sexuality during adolescence. It takes an enormous amount of courage to finally tell your parents something so profound about yourself when you're not sure how they'll react, especially if you're terrified they'll respond negatively. Regardless of how you feel about your child's revelation, it's essential that you respond in a nonjudgmental way. Tell them how grateful you are that they've shared this with you, and that you know it may have been hard to do so.

If you're confused, upset, disappointed, or angry about what your child has disclosed, try to hold these feelings in while your child is describing their sexual orientation or gender identity to you. It took time for your child to adjust to this new understanding of themselves, and it will take time for you to adapt, too.

Regardless of your feelings, remind yourself that your child is still the same person they've always been. They haven't suddenly become a stranger. All that's changed is that you now know something about them that you didn't know or weren't sure about before. Now you know your kid better than you did before. That's something to be happy about.

Don't try to think back about signals you missed or berate yourself for having failed to see them. Remember, someone's sexual orientation or gender identity isn't necessarily reflected in how they look or behave. You didn't miss any telltale signs. You can't deduce a person's sexual orientation or gender identity from their actions or interests. And don't say anything to your child like "I always knew this about you." That would just make them feel awkward for not telling you earlier.

After they've finished their revelation, embrace them and reassure them that you love them for who they are and will always be there to support and care for them. If they mention that they're currently in a relationship with someone, tell them you'd like to meet that person, and welcome them into your life whenever they and their partner feel comfortable making the introduction. It may take a while before all of you are ready to take this next step, so don't rush it if you, your child, or your child's partner is uncomfortable.

Parents often have questions they'd like to ask in the wake of such a revelation, like how long their kid has known this about themselves and whether they're open about their sexual orientation and identity with others. Feel free to ask questions, as long as you do so in a respectful, sincere way. Frankly, many young adults would think it was odd if their parents *didn't* have questions, and they might misinterpret their silence as disapproval.

If, after a while, you're still having a tough time understanding and accepting your child's sexual orientation or gender identity, there are organizations that help families with this issue. One excellent source of support and information is the national organization PFLAG (www.pflag.org), which has local chapters all over the country. Reach out to them if you need guidance or support or think it would be helpful to speak with other families who've faced, or who are facing, similar challenges.

Young adulthood is a time when many parents discover things about their child's sexuality that come as a surprise. It's also a time when parents learn more—for better and for worse—about their child's taste in romantic partners.

## Your Child's Choice of a Partner

If your kid is typical, they probably had at least one serious romance during high school, so by now you've had the experience of meeting and perhaps getting to know someone they were dating. But when they were a teenager, you probably assumed that any romance they had wouldn't last too long.

The odds of marrying a college boyfriend or girlfriend aren't high, either. Only about one-fourth of today's married people met their spouse in college. These days, the average person is likely to have had many different romantic relationships by the time they're twenty-five. It's not that people in their teens and early twenties are promiscuous—it's just that they rarely expect their early romances to turn into marriages, so they stay involved with someone they're seeing until one or both of them lose interest, at which point they move on.

It's far more common for people to meet their future spouse sometime in their late twenties or early thirties. If you have a child this age who's in a serious relationship, there's a reasonable possibility they'll end up marrying this person. According to recent surveys, the average age at which people met their future spouse is twenty-seven—a little younger than this among women, and a little older among men.

That's exactly what Marsha and Alan had been hoping for after they got to know their son's girlfriend. Tom, who was thirty-one when he met Liz, had waited three months before he introduced her to his parents. By then, the couple knew they were serious enough to take this step. Because Tom's parents lived nearby, they got together with the couple regularly, and the four of them enjoyed spending time together.

Tom's parents had usually liked the women Tom dated—the one exception was a woman Tom met online and went out with for a few months before introducing her over dinner at a local restaurant. After the foursome had finished eating and the young couple said good night and left, Alan handed the bill back to the waiter and asked him to add a scotch on the rocks to the tab. "What a piece of work," he said to his wife as he sipped his drink. "Can you believe how argumentative she was? I thought I was going to explode. It was all I could do to control myself."

"It was pretty obvious," Marsha said. "I'm sure Tom could see it."

Tom's parents never needed to say a word to him about the dinner—he stopped seeing the woman a few days later. Although parental disapproval occasionally intensifies a couple's commitment to each other, this so-called Romeo and Juliet effect is the exception, not the rule. Few young people deliberately choose a romantic partner they know their parents don't care for.

Liz could not have been more different. She was intelligent, graceful, and charming. Marsha and Alan could see how much Liz cared for their son, and they really hoped she would be the one.

They were disappointed when Tom called and told them he and Liz had decided to break up. "It's hard to explain," Tom said, aware of how much his parents liked Liz. "We got along really well, but there just wasn't enough passion there for me. We'll be better off as friends than as a couple." His parents said they had very much enjoyed getting to know Liz, but that they certainly understood Tom's feelings.

"What a shame," Marsha said to her husband later. "She's a really lovely girl. But if it wasn't working, it wasn't working. I trust Tom's instincts. And he's the one who needs to be happy. I'm sure someone else will come along. He doesn't seem to have any problems meeting people."

❧

It's easy for parents to keep their opinion to themselves when their child breaks things off with someone they're fond of, but it's much harder to remain quiet when they're sure their child is making a mistake and dating someone they don't like or find unsuitable in some way. No parent wants to see their child stuck in a bad relationship. But if they speak up and their child ignores their advice, they run the risk of creating distance between them and their child.

You've no doubt met people in your child's life you don't like very much, but there usually isn't any reason to voice your displeasure if the person is your child's friend, coworker, or someone they've been dating casually. Your child can sense these things and over time will probably stop bringing around people you don't care for, so even if they remain a part of your child's life, they don't become part of yours. It's very different when the person is your child's potential spouse or partner and you'll almost certainly need to figure out a way of coexisting.

If your child is younger than twenty-five and dating someone you can't abide, it's probably safe to keep your mouth shut unless they say they're intending to make a long-term commitment to each other. You should treat the person cordially, but there's no reason to voice your opinion about them. Your child knows the difference between how you behave when you like someone and how you act when you don't. If you have a good relationship with your child, it's unlikely they'll plan to marry someone they know you dislike. You should be more concerned about a potential partner if your child is in their mid- or late thirties because at this age their eagerness to find a long-term partner may impair their judgment.

Sometimes you know why you disapprove of someone your child is dating, but often it's just a bad feeling that's hard to articulate. In these cases, it's important to stop and ask yourself just what's bothering you. It may help to discuss how you feel with your partner or a friend, because putting your vague impressions into words and then hearing someone else's reaction to them will help you gain clarity.

Perhaps you don't care for their personality—you find them dull, brash, crass, or socially awkward. Maybe they're interested in things you couldn't care less about, uninterested in the things that excite you, or both—what on earth will the two of you talk about? Maybe their ethnic, religious, or socioeconomic background isn't what you had imagined for your child's partner. Perhaps you're bothered by the fact that your child intends to marry someone who had been married before, especially if they have children from their prior marriage—you may wonder if your kid is ready to become a parent to someone else's child, which can be a difficult challenge. Maybe you can tolerate your child's partner, but you can't stand their family.

If the reason for your disapproval is something that doesn't pose any threat to your child's well-being, you should do and say nothing. It will only jeopardize your relationship with your child. It doesn't matter whether you're right or wrong about their partner. How the couple feel about each other is what matters. Besides, having been raised by you and probably sharing some of your values and world-view, your child probably sees some of the same qualities in their partner that you do but isn't bothered by them, or sees positive traits that outweigh the negative ones. It may just take some time for you to see the person through your kid's eyes rather than your own. Try to do this before forming a final opinion.

Moreover, if you express your misgivings to your child, you're putting them in a difficult position. How are they supposed to act when you're all together? If their partner tells your child that they sense you don't like them, what should your child say? And suppose their partner reaches a point where they issue an ultimatum: "It's me or them—you have to choose."

You may think you're doing your child a favor by speaking up before their relationship gets any more serious, but in fact it may be just the opposite.

It's a different matter if you can point to something specific about a potential mate that's likely to harm your child. Here you should be concerned about worrisome patterns of behavior like emotional abuse, substance abuse, philandering, or refusal to work or look for a job. Tell your child they should not get into a long-term relationship with this person until they've demanded and seen a lasting change in their behavior. If your child disregards your advice and stays in the relationship, there's nothing you can do, but if problems arise after the couple is married, you can help your child deal with them (see "Helping Your Child Handle Conflicts with Their Partner" on page 154).

But even if you adore your child's partner, if they decide to get married, you're in for a new set of challenges around the wedding—and beyond.

## The Member of the Wedding

Weddings are supposed to be joyous occasions, and most of the time they are. But, like many events that involve a lot of people, require many decisions, evoke strong emotions, and tax people's time and resources, planning a wedding provides dozens of opportunities for disagreement.

In thinking about the wedding, it's important to distinguish between the marriage and the ceremony. There's no doubt about whose *marriage* it is, and the couple should determine what kind of ceremony they want, as it reflects the ideals and goals they intend to bring to their marriage. So they should decide who will officiate, how they each dress, and what vows they exchange. But a potential source of tension you should confront before any decisions about the day are made is to clarify whose *wedding* it is—the couple's or their families'.

This viewpoint varies considerably between cultures and generations, where in some cases a wedding celebration is understood by everyone in attendance as an event (or events) hosted by one or both of the couple's families. In this case, the hosts of the reception are the ones to decide what the event will be, because it reflects on the *family*. This perspective may sound old-fashioned, but it's a deeply held view in many cultures, especially those that place a strong emphasis on "familism"—the belief that the family is more important than any of its members.

In other cases, the wedding celebration is viewed as an occasion that reflects mainly on the couple, and it's the two people getting married who decide what the affair will be like. It's their way of making a statement to others about *themselves*. This is the view that's often taken for granted in modern-day America, but that would seem bizarre, if not selfish and disrespectful, in many other parts of the world.

Given the extent to which we are a nation of immigrants and the increasing number of marriages between people from different ethnic backgrounds, a disparity in perspective between couples and their parents—or between the people getting married—isn't unusual. There is no simple way to resolve this issue other than by talking about it openly and honestly. One possibility might be multiple celebrations, one hosted and planned by parents and one hosted and planned by the couple.

There is no agreed-upon set of rules anymore that dictate who pays for which parts of the celebration. The traditional view has been that the bride's parents pay for the wedding and the groom's parents pay for the celebration that precedes it, like a rehearsal or welcome dinner or reception, as well as the couple's honeymoon. But many families don't follow this model, and now that people are marrying later—when they themselves have more money—more couples either pay for their own wedding events or share the cost with their parents. Moreover, given the increase in same-sex marriages, the bride/groom distinction with respect to financing the wedding no longer makes sense.

Deciding how the cost of the wedding and other events will be shared is best done by the couple in consultation with each of their families separately, which avoids any awkwardness caused by everyone discovering that one family is paying substantially more than the other. This way, only the bride and groom will know what each family is contributing. If this is how your child and their partner plan to proceed, don't ask what the other parents are contributing. Families don't all have the same resources—and even if they have comparable incomes, parents who are helping to finance four children's weddings are in a different position from those who have only one child's wedding to think about. If you're offering to help cover the cost of the wedding, you're giving the couple a gift, and what you give them shouldn't depend on what they're getting from anyone else.

Before discussing finances, the couple should rough out what they want to do and gather some information about the likely costs of various components. They can then consult separately with each of their parents and find out how much of a contribution they can make. The couple can then calculate what they can afford, revise their plans if necessary, and figure out the best way to use each family's contribution. They might decide to ask one family to pay for certain parts of the celebration and the other family to pay for others, or they may suggest that all the contributions be pooled and used without specifying who's paying for what.

How any contribution you make is used is something for you and the couple to discuss. If you agree that the money you're giving them is designated for a specific event, like the wedding reception or the rehearsal dinner, the details of the event are best decided jointly between you and the couple, unless you all agree differently. If you disagree about minor details—like the color of the table linens— defer to the couple's preference, if only to minimize their stress. But if your difference is about something significant—who is on the invitation list, for example—try to resolve it using collaborative problem-solving (see chapter 2, "Resolving Disputes Constructively" on page 40). A wedding celebration is different than a party you are throwing where you're deciding all of the specifics, though, because a wedding is often part of a series of events, some of which are being planned by the couple and the other set of parents. For example, if you're hosting the wedding reception and the other parents are hosting the welcome dinner, the couple will need to coordinate the plans. They probably don't want the same menu served at both events.

When you're meeting with the wedding couple to plan an event you're hosting, whether you are helping to pay for it or not, try to be flexible. Organizing a wedding is stressful, so don't add to the pressures the couple are already dealing with. Hopefully, you all know each other well enough by now to come up with a schedule of events that's acceptable to everyone. You might have an initial conversation for everybody to describe what they have in mind. Then you can all take a few days to mull things over and reconvene to see if there is a way to satisfy everyone's wishes, at least partially.

Paying for wedding expenses isn't the only potential source of prenuptial tension between parents and child. There also may be differences of opinion about who's invited to the ceremony and reception; how to handle potential problems (as well as finances) when one or both sets of parents are divorced or remarried and not on friendly terms with their ex-spouse; which people are asked to toast the couple, and in what order; the seating arrangements; and the accommodations if the event is a destination wedding held at a resort or in some exotic location. If so, the couple should make the initial decisions and run them by each set of parents for their approval.

If you disagree with some element of the plan, voice your concern and suggest how it might be addressed. As the parents of the bride or groom, you should speak up, regardless of whether and how much you're contributing financially. Make sure to do it well in advance of the wedding so everything can be settled before the big day. Your family may not come from a traditional culture, but all parents deserve to be respected, especially at their child's wedding. If you aren't treated well on the first day of your child's marriage, you may face bigger problems ahead. After the wedding is over and the couple has returned from their honeymoon, if they took one, voice your concerns about how you've been treated and straighten things out now. It's best to do this with both your child and their partner present so that everyone knows your concerns.

## How Your Child's Intimate Relationship
## May Change Your Relationship with Them

It's often said that when your child gets married, you aren't losing them but gaining an in-law. This is only partly true. When a child marries or becomes involved in a committed long-term relationship, their parent doesn't *lose* them, but their relationship changes in ways that may feel like a loss. (Although I may use the words "married," "spouse," and "in-laws," what I have to say here refers to couples who are legally married as well as those who are not.)

When our kids form attachments to others, they become more emotionally autonomous from us. The intimacy that defines a romantic relationship in adolescence is different from anything they've experienced previously. Knowing they can depend on a boyfriend or girlfriend to provide love and support makes adolescents feel more confident and mature, which gives them the wherewithal to individuate from their parents. A similar process takes place when a young adult gets married.

Changes in our relationships alter how we see ourselves, which in turn changes how we interact with others. Forming new intimate relationships lessens the young adult's need to rely on their parents for emotional support, which lets them become more distant from their parents. This is an essential part of developing autonomy from parents (see chapter 1, "Respecting Your Child's Autonomy" on page 17). It would be very surprising if your relationship with your child *didn't* change after they got married.

In fact, if they didn't pull away from you somewhat after making a commitment, I'd wonder whether the relationship is giving them what they need emotionally. A new marriage shouldn't sever a person's ties with their parents, but if a newlywed is usually turning to their parents rather than their partner during difficult times, something may be amiss. Your child has a finite amount of emotional energy to invest in their close relationships, and once they're married, they should be investing most of it in their spouse.

Across many different realms, your child and their partner must make decisions they didn't have to face before they moved in together. Some of these decisions are pedestrian—how they furnish their place, what kind of car they buy, where to buy their groceries. But others are consequential—what home they decide to purchase, how they raise their child, where they spend the holidays. You may learn of decisions that surprise you because they don't seem like choices your child would make and because they depart from what you would advise.

In cases like this, try not to be annoyed. For one thing, you don't know what decisions the couple has made that were dictated by your child's preferences. For another, keeping the peace with their mate is more important than pleasing you—as it should be. One of the most important aspects of living with someone is allowing that person to influence and change you.

The fact that some of your child's opinions differ from yours more than you'd like isn't a rejection of your taste, ideas, or values. It's their acknowledgment that there is someone in their life whose opinions matter more than yours do. If you have to hold your nose and look away from time to time, that's a small price to pay for your child's marital happiness. And you may well end up liking the decisions that were influenced by their partner and reconsidering your own opinion. You may have never cared much for a particular style of furniture, but when you visit your child and sit on a chair their partner chose, you may find it comfortable, even if doesn't please your eye.

Another factor to consider when pondering the impact of your child's marriage on your relationship with them is whether you're their mother or father, and whether the child is a son or a daughter. In many cases, marriage makes mothers and daughters closer, because in most families, women are what are called "kinkeepers"—the people who manage relationships within the family and the family's relationships with the outside world.

A kinkeeper's aim is to make sure family members get along. In order to serve this end, mothers and daughters tend to stay in closer touch after a marriage than do fathers and their children or mothers and sons, because when you both are kinkeepers, you will probably speak more frequently than the other dyads about family plans and dynamics, some of which will be new, like managing people's preferences for how to spend important holidays.

From the moment they're born, females are more social and more socially skilled than males on average, and this is evident throughout life. Girls generally begin talking before boys, and girls are more advanced than boys in all aspects of language development, including putting words together to form phrases and sentences. Girls are also better than boys in nonverbal aspects of communication, including making eye contact, using gestures, and social referencing—picking up cues by watching other people's expressions and paying attention to their emotions. Girls' advantages in social skills persist throughout childhood and adolescence, shape the ways women interact with others, and play out in the greater emotional intensity of girls' and women's friendships and family relationships. Not only are women better at communicating, but they're also more socially astute and more interested in relationships, which makes them ideal kinkeepers. If you're a mother whose daughter is about to get married, you'll likely enjoy a closer bond with them than you had before the wedding.

If you're a father, your relationship with your married child, whatever their gender, may become more distant, and you may find that you must work to regain your former intimacy, like calling just to chat or suggesting activities to share. Doing things from time to time alone with your child will do more to strengthen your bond than doing things that also include your respective partners. Those group activities are important, of course, and your separate times with your child should be seen as supplements to them, not replacements.

But if you're a mother whose son has just married a woman, you may find yourself a little jealous of the amount of time his wife and her mother spend talking and texting compared to you and your son. And this will only increase if your son and his wife become parents, because having a child creates yet another set of relationships for your daughter-in-law and her mother to discuss and manage.

One way to stay connected to your child after they marry is to develop a strong emotional bond with their partner. Indeed, one of the many benefits of a good relationship with your child's partner is that it strengthens your relationship with your child. Plus, their partner may also become a very good friend in their own right, and you may enjoy spending time with your in-law as much as you do with your child.

## Getting Along with Your Child's Partner

Developing a good relationship with your in-law is crucial to the quality of your relationship with your child, and it will be even more important if you become a grandparent.

After the marriage, your relationship with your child's partner will unfold in three stages: *honeymoon*, *appraisal*, and *equilibrium*. If you become a grandparent, your relationship with your child's partner will enter a fourth phase, a topic I discuss in chapter 8.

*Honeymoon.* Early on in your child's marriage, your relationship with their partner differs from your other family relationships. They may be unfamiliar with your family's norms, expectations, or traditions, some of which they may not care for. They're not someone you chose to have in your life. They're in your life because your child chose them, and even if you weren't happy with the choice, the two of you need to get along. Moreover, you can't end your relationship with them because you've had a falling out or you feel mistreated— because any attempt to end it will result in unpleasant and lasting ramifications for the entire family.

A relationship between a parent and a child-in-law entails high stakes. The costs of letting it deteriorate are great, as is the need to get things off on the right foot.

This dynamic works in the other direction as well. In most cases, at least at the beginning of a marriage, your child's partner wants to get along with you. If you have a good relationship with your child, your new in-law will likely want to make you glad to have them in your life. It's a high-stakes relationship for them, too.

During the honeymoon stage, both of you are likely to be on your best behavior. You may go out of your way to be thoughtful and complimentary—congratulating them on their accomplishments, staying on the phone with them when you've called to speak to your child, or texting a link to something you think they'll enjoy. If you live nearby, suggest an occasional outing for just the two of you so you can get to know each other better.

Your child wants things to work between you and their partner, too, because any sort of rift will affect them. If they sense that things have gotten off to a bad start, they'll probably want to do what they can to fix what's wrong as soon as possible (assuming they're aware of this, which isn't always the case). They may go out of their way to organize family activities in which you and their partner will enjoy yourselves, hoping that good feelings created by the experience will influence your general feelings about your nascent bond. After a few months, when the honeymoon is over, things may get more complicated, as your relationship with your child-in-law begins to shift from mutual and largely uncritical acceptance to a more cautious and objective evaluation of each other. You've now entered the appraisal stage of the relationship.

*Appraisal.* In high-stakes relationships, where the costs of a misunderstanding are potentially serious, people are especially vigilant. They're likely to guard against doing anything that might upset the other person, but they're also extra sensitive to the other person's slights and snubs, which, unless they are frequent, are probably unintentional. Both of you are trying to be on your best behavior, but at the same time you each may be on the lookout for signs of rejection or disrespect. Whether a slight is inadvertent or intended, though, if you feel badly treated so soon into the marriage, say something to your child in private to nip this in the bud. You may expect to get a thank-you note after giving a gift or treating someone to a special occasion, for example, but your child's partner may not be accustomed to doing this, and if you mention this to your child, they can let their partner know it's important to you.

Neither you nor your child's partner wants to be seen as responsible for a problem between the two of you. The last thing either of you want is for your child to accuse one of you of making life difficult for the other, and by extension, for themselves. If this happens, your child may have an awkward conversation separately with each of you, the essence of which is "I know you two have gotten off to a bad start, but it's important to me that you find a way to comfortably coexist, because it's just too difficult for all of us if you don't."

At the beginning of the appraisal stage there can be a fair amount of tiptoeing as you and your child-in-law feel each other out and learn each other's trigger points. There's no way you can possibly know so early in your relationship what's going to annoy them and which annoyances will linger as grudges. It's a process of interpersonal trial and error, and it's only a matter of time before one of you inadvertently upsets the other.

If you feel you've been treated badly, you should discuss the situation with a friend or with your partner before saying anything to your child about it, to verify you haven't misinterpreted or overreacted. It's probably best at this stage to let the occasional slight pass without comment. You've probably made a few mistakes of your own that you're unaware of. Just give this new relationship some time to find its footing.

Gaining a sense of who your child-in-law really is and how best to interact with them will be a challenge for both of you, but it's probably going to be harder for you than for them. They have the benefit of a live-in coach—your child—to recommend how they should behave with you. Before an evening together, your child can suggest things their partner should say or do, and caution against words or actions that might cause trouble.

It's less likely you'll be coached by your child in the same way because there's an inherent status difference between you and your child-in-law. You and your child's partner are each expected to be kind and gracious, but your child's partner is also expected to show you the respect a parent is entitled to. It's unlikely your child will take you aside, as they might do with their spouse, and explicitly encourage you to change your behavior. (That may come later, but seldom early in the marriage.)

One issue that sometimes arises during this stage of your relationship is whether to communicate with your child about their partner or with their partner about your child. Until you determine how intimate your relationship with your child-in-law will be, if you have concerns about their behavior or well-being, you should start by asking your child for their advice on how best to handle it.

Let's say your daughter-in-law seems depressed. It may be too early in your relationship to express your concerns to her directly— you don't know yet what her normal emotional ups and downs are, and what looks to you like depression may just be a mood that she sometimes falls into that your child knows and understands. Going directly to her, even to empathize, may make her feel self-conscious or annoyed. It's wiser to share your concerns with your child. They may explain that it's nothing to worry about, that they're aware of their wife's depression and have spoken with her about it, or that they think you should speak to her directly. Trust your child's judgment.

If you're worried about your child, speak to them without involving their partner. The only exception might be a situation in which you feel your child is in some sort of danger of harming themselves— if they've said something about taking their life or if you think they've developed a substance abuse problem—and they didn't respond when you first expressed your concern and suggested they seek help. At that point, share your concerns with your child's partner, who may have more success when they approach their spouse.

How long the appraisal stage lasts will depend on how much time you spend with the couple. This will differ between those who live near each other and those who are too far away for frequent get-togethers. Because people often behave differently when their meetings are overextended visits—some are on their best behavior, while others don't do well either as visitors or hosts—if this is how you get to know your child-in-law, you may not get a complete picture until after several stays together.

It's possible, although not ideal, to get to know each other through telephone or video calls between visits. I'd resist using email or texting to achieve this end, though. As we've all learned, sentiments that are written rather than spoken are often misinterpreted because so much of what we glean about someone's emotional state, intentions, etc., is picked up from tone of voice, facial expressions, and gestures. Once you and your child-in-law have established a strong bond, it's fine to communicate electronically.

*Equilibrium.* After you've spent enough time together under different circumstances—dinners at home or in restaurants, outings, holiday gatherings, extended stays, vacations—you and your child-in-law will probably have settled into a relationship whose contours won't change much unless something momentous happens, like a divorce, the arrival of a grandchild, or a serious illness in the family.

It's hard to say in advance what your relationship will be like, and there's no single "right" way to relate to them. You may become fast friends with them and spend a lot of time together visiting museums, hiking, fly-fishing, baking bread, watching sports, or whatever you enjoy doing together. The two of you may even develop a close bond that's independent from your relationship with your child, and you may be in more frequent contact with each other than you are with your kid. If you're especially friendly with your child's partner and have known each other for a long enough time, you may be comfortable talking openly with each other without having to rely on your child as a go-between.

Other parents enjoy their child-in-law's company at family get-togethers, but don't see or speak to each other much between these gatherings. Still others behave cordially when they see their child's partner and happily make small talk when they find themselves sitting next to each other at dinner, but don't seek much more from the relationship than this. And some children and their mother- or father-in-law tacitly agree to tolerate each other and avoid stepping on each other's toes.

Maybe one of you had hoped your relationship would be closer than it is, but parents and their children-in-law just need to get along well enough to keep the peace. After enough time has gone by, you should accept things as they are and not try to change anything.

No law or custom says that a parent and their child-in-law must like each other. If the two of you do, you're very fortunate, and every so often you should tell them how lucky you feel.

## Helping Your Child Handle Conflicts with Their Partner

All couples argue—on average, several times a month. Conflict between your child and their partner is seldom something to worry about, and almost never something in which you should intervene. If you sense that the couple isn't getting along, but neither your child nor their partner has mentioned it to you, don't comment. Arguments between people in a serious long-term relationship usually result from miscommunication or a misunderstanding about something relatively minor, like an errand one of them forgot to run. (Contrary to conventional wisdom, sex and money are *not* what couples usually fight about.) This is especially true early in the relationship, after the honeymoon is over but before a couple has figured out how to work out their differences constructively. Seeing a new couple squabble doesn't usually indicate that the marriage is in jeopardy.

If you're present while an argument between your child and their partner breaks out, or if you walk in on a fight, excuse yourself and let them settle things on their own. Say something like "I think it's better if you two work this out in private. Let's get together at a better time." Don't comment on it the next time you see or talk to each other. Doing so may only revive the disagreement.

One exception to this guidance is if you see any physical violence or have good reason to think violence is imminent. This may happen if one or both members of the couple have been drinking, which is often the case when an argument escalates into violence. If that happens, you should do what you can to separate the couple, stop the fight, and remain present until things have calmed down. If you know there's a firearm in the house, call the domestic violence hotline (1-800-799-SAFE), leave immediately, and take one member of the couple with you if you can. More than a quarter of all homicides in the United States are related to domestic violence, and the presence of a gun in the home substantially increases the likelihood a fight will be deadly.

When your child is going through a tough time in their relationship, they may turn to you. If they do, listen nonjudgmentally and provide emotional support. Ask questions to better understand the situation, but don't give advice on whether or how to repair a damaged relationship unless you're asked for it. Even then, you should focus on helping your child think of ways to settle the conflict constructively rather than trying to diagnose its cause based solely on their point of view (there are usually two sides to a disagreement). The key to a solid marriage isn't avoiding conflict, but figuring out how to stop it from escalating and how to resolve it. If it's early in the couple's marriage, don't be dismissive ("I think you're making too much of this—all couples argue from time to time"), but don't overreact, either. Instead, empathize with the *couple* rather than your child ("This must be difficult for the two of you").

In the unlikely event your child's partner comes to you to talk about a disagreement the couple is having, behave just as you would if you had been approached by your child: listen nonjudgmentally and empathize. Although it may be tempting to side with your child, don't. Most bonds are strong enough to withstand occasional rough patches, and if your child's relationship emerges from one and returns to normal, you want to be on good terms with their partner. Siding with your child might contribute to further conflict.

If you know the couple is arguing frequently, intensely, or irreconcilably, suggest they try couples counseling. This can be especially helpful if their problems are the result of frequent miscommunication.

※

Divorce in America is a lot less common today than it was at its peak in the late 1970s. Most experts attribute the decline to the fact that people are waiting longer to get married and using the extra time to be more selective in choosing a spouse. Divorce is particularly unlikely among college graduates. About 80 percent of college-educated women and two-thirds of college-educated men stay married for at least twenty years, compared to fewer than half of those with less education. This is true for two main reasons. First, the earlier a couple marries, the greater their chances of divorcing, and the age at which people marry is highly correlated with how far they went in school. Second, a main contributor to divorce is financial strain, and people with more education generally have more money. Interestingly, despite all the stress caused by the COVID-19 pandemic, divorce became even less common than it was before, with many couples saying they grew closer during the crisis.

If your child is in their thirties, they're at the age when the chances of divorce are greatest—but remember, if they graduated from college, divorce is unlikely at any age.

Divorce is most common during the first two years of marriage and again around the fifth anniversary. After five years, which for many couples is after about seven years of living together (giving some credence to the notion of a "seven-year itch"), the odds of divorcing steadily decline. We can assume that early divorces are due to bad decisions, but the reason for the second bump is unclear. Marital satisfaction declines steadily after the first few months, even among couples who are basically happy. After about five years, it's likely that couples make a decision to either live with a less-than-perfect relationship or end it.

Although divorce is less common today than at any time since the 1970s, there's always a chance your child's marriage won't work out. Going through a divorce is stressful, but the stress is temporary, and ending an unhappy marriage is far preferable to staying in one, so encourage your child to try to work it out where appropriate, but don't try to talk your child into staying in a marriage they can't stand. Moreover, the majority of people who divorce in their thirties remarry, usually within four years. If your kid gets divorced, they probably won't live alone for the rest of their life.

If your child does get divorced, you may need to provide assistance with finances, housing, childcare, and legal expenses. More important than these types of assistance, however, is your continuing presence in your child's life. A divorce often leads to a loss of social connections, because when people separate from a spouse, they may lose contact with their former in-laws (with whom they may have been friendly) as well as friends who remain connected to their ex but not them. Studies of people's mental health following a divorce clearly show that social support from their family is a significant buffer against depression, distress, and insomnia, and a significant contributor to happiness and life satisfaction.

If your divorcing child is a parent, their child is probably still pretty young, and younger children are far less likely to develop psychological problems as a result of their parents' breakup than are preteens or teenagers. Regardless of your grandchild's age, the quality of their relationship with each of their parents after a divorce is much more important for the child's psychological well-being than the specific custody arrangements, so do what you can to avoid enmeshing the child in an angry custody dispute. For your grandchild's sake, try to steer your child and their ex away from a contentious custody battle by reminding them that how they interact with each other affects their youngster's psychological well-being. And make sure that you don't make a combative situation worse by fanning the flames.

Sometimes a divorcing couple gets so caught up in their own antipathy for each other that they forget about what's in the child's best interest. Do everything you can to encourage your child and their ex to maintain an amicable relationship and shield their child from their disputes. Exposure to marital and postmarital conflict is far more damaging to children's mental health than their parents' separation or divorce. Staying together for the sake of the child does not benefit the child and can actually cause harm if their parents are fighting all the time.

If your grandchild had a good relationship with your child before the divorce, it's important that they remain a part of your grandchild's life, even if they don't have custody. If you can help make this happen, by arranging joint activities that include you, your child, and your grandchild, you should.

Staying in close contact with your grandchild is also important for their well-being. If your child and their ex-spouse are estranged and your child's ex tries to prohibit you from seeing your grandchild, discuss the matter with them and explain why you think being in your grandchild's life is important to you and the child. See if they'll change their mind and agree to periodic planned visits according to a schedule you all can agree on. If that fails, you can petition the court for visitation rights, but you'll have to demonstrate that your continued contact with your grandchild will be beneficial to the youngster. Grandparents' rights to spend time with their grandchildren following a divorce vary from state to state.

Studies of divorce consistently show that the difficulties faced by the divorcees and, if they are parents, their children, are usually temporary, disappearing within two years after the breakup. If you're going through a tough time as a result of your child's divorce, it will also likely be temporary, and things will improve for you as they improve for your child and grandchild. Supporting them emotionally and financially, if they're in need and you can afford it, will help them recover faster. When you're feeling upset about what your child and grandchild have gone through, remember to tell yourself that living in a bad marriage wasn't good for either of them. In most cases, there is light at the end of the tunnel.

## CHAPTER SEVEN

# Flourishing or Floundering?

## Is My Child Floundering?

As you watch your child's forays into the worlds of college, career, and romantic commitment, you're probably wondering whether they're on the right tracks toward completing their formal education, succeeding in the world of work, and developing a gratifying intimate relationship with a life partner. Because the timetable of adulthood has changed so much since you were that age, it's often hard to know whether your kid is making progress toward a rewarding adult life.

This is why one of the most common questions I hear from parents of young adults is how to tell if their child is floundering.

A young adult is floundering when they appear to be rudderless, struggling to define a path they hope to follow and to make progress along it. It's marked by false starts and haphazard decision-making about school, work, relationships, and/or living arrangements— an inability to find one's footing in one or more of these realms. Typically, young adults who are floundering feel restless, helpless, pessimistic, disconnected, and dejected. Some seem stuck, mired in indecision. Others seem frenetic, bouncing from one ill-considered decision to another. Either way, a young person who's floundering isn't making progress.

Flourishing is the opposite of floundering. Some years ago, my colleagues and I developed a model of flourishing, which we called EPOCH, an acronym of the names of the five qualities that comprise the construct:

- Engagement (the ability to stay absorbed and focused in a chosen activity)
- Perseverance (grit and determination in the face of obstacles)
- Optimism (hopefulness and confidence about the future)
- Connectedness (having satisfying relationships with others)
- Happiness (feeling content with life)

If your adult child has these qualities, they're flourishing. Even if they haven't yet accomplished their goals, they have the psychological strengths they need to succeed.

It's possible to flounder in one life domain or in many, or flounder in some respects but flourish in others. I've known young adults who couldn't figure out what career to pursue but were happily involved in a committed romance. I've known others who were happy with their work life but had trouble finding a romantic partner despite desperately wanting one. And I've known some whose entire life lacked direction.

Because floundering has both objective and subjective elements (that is, how someone's life is unfolding and how they feel about it), it's important to look at both before deciding whether your child is in trouble. And don't project your own feelings of concern or anxiety onto your child. Just because you were unhappy being single in your thirties doesn't mean your child feels the same way about being unattached. And just because they want to change careers doesn't mean they're pessimistic about their future.

Moreover, just because your child hasn't progressed along what you consider a normal timetable doesn't mean they're floundering. Floundering has nothing to do with being "late" in moving into the roles of adulthood. It's more a function of uncertainty, indecisiveness, and distress—signs of their struggle to figure out who they are.

As I've stressed, early adulthood doesn't unfold along the same timetable today as it did a generation ago. You may think your kid is taking too long to get married and start a family, but people are getting married later these days than when you were growing up, and many young adults are happy to be single and childless. You may wonder why they have been in college for six years and don't have a degree to show for it, but it takes longer for people to graduate now than it did a generation ago. It might seem like it's taking a long time for your kid's career to get off the ground, but this isn't unusual in today's labor market. You may be upset to see your adult child move back home, but this is a very reasonable tack to take if they're trying to save money for a down payment on a place of their own.

Four observations frequently trigger parents' concerns that their adult child is floundering: they seem to be taking too long to finish their education, they aren't following a clear career path, they haven't settled into a committed romantic relationship, or they've had to move back home after living independently. But these don't necessarily indicate floundering, because factors outside their control may have impacted their situation. That's why it's important that parents understand what factors may contribute to each of these situations and how best to respond.

## The Perpetual Student

For parents and children alike, graduation is one of life's most significant milestones. Outside of religious ceremonies, modern society has few other rites of passage. Unfortunately, some parents don't get to witness these transitions because their child drops out of school before completing a degree. Other parents are deprived, if perhaps temporarily, because their child seems to be taking too long to finish their education. They may wonder—especially if they're still paying tuition bills—if their child will be in school forever.

Some parents worry this is a sign their kid is floundering, but this isn't always the case. "Perpetual students" fall into two broad categories: those who take a long time to finish their undergraduate degree, and those who graduate from college (in whatever amount of time it takes) but continue their studies in graduate or professional schools, perhaps accumulating (or trying to accumulate) multiple degrees.

Let's start with the undergraduates who remain in college for a long time.

It's more helpful to look at scholastic floundering in a kid's early twenties as a mental health problem rather than a departure from what you, as a parent, believe is the "right" timetable for reaching that milestone. Rather than watching the clock, you should ask yourself why your child isn't completing their degree along the same schedule as other students their age. Is your child apprehensive about leaving school and starting the next phase of life? That sounds like floundering. But some students are genuinely trying to finish within a reasonable amount of time but face institutional hurdles that interfere with their progress, like their college failing to offer required courses often enough for students to complete their degree on time. This is very different.

You might be surprised to learn that the average time it takes students who attend what we typically consider to be four-year schools to complete a bachelor's degree has increased over the past generation to about five years. Fewer than 45 percent finish in four years, and an additional 20 percent within five. Some students take considerably longer than that to finish: about one-third take six years or more, and one-fourth take seven years or more. It's too soon to quantify how the pandemic further affected graduation rates and timetables, but it undoubtedly disrupted many students' schooling and increased mental health problems among young adults in general, either of which could have contributed to a student taking longer to finish school than expected.

Many reasons college takes longer to finish are beyond students' control and not at all indicative of floundering. For example, during the pandemic, many colleges switched from in-person to remote instruction for most of their classes. Many rising freshmen who were hoping for the traditional college experience—living in a dorm, dining with classmates, meeting with professors in person, and socializing with their peers—decided to postpone college until things were back to normal. This isn't floundering.

I also wouldn't consider a student to be floundering if their school doesn't offer courses required for graduation often enough to accommodate everyone who needs them. This sort of shortfall forces many students to stay in school longer than they anticipated. This has become a widespread problem among colleges and universities whose enrollments have increased faster than they've been able to hire additional instructors or find extra classroom space. Nor would I view a student as floundering if they were forced to take time off from school for financial reasons or because they enlisted in the military, became a parent, or had to set college aside temporarily or attend part-time while they worked to help their family stay financially afloat.

To determine if your kid is floundering academically, you should look at the timing, frequency, and impulsivity of the decisions they've made that have increased how long it will take them to graduate. Some drag college out well beyond four or five years because they change majors so often that they can't complete their degree requirements in less time. Some transfer to different schools multiple times, which will delay graduation if some of the course credits they accumulated aren't transferable. Some may change majors *and* schools, which postpones graduation even more. These are all signs of floundering.

Other young adults drop in and out of college, intending to eventually finish their degree, but always finding some excuse to take a break—mainly to do not much more than laze around. Some may prolong their education simply because they like not having to work, socializing on campus, and carrying a light course load while their parents foot the bill. This, too, is floundering. If this sounds like your child, it would be far less expensive for them to take a leave of absence from college and move back home—but some young people may find this arrangement too restrictive, and some parents may be less than happy to have their student live with them (see "When Your Child Moves Back Home" on page 185).

It's understandable to sympathize with a student who wants to change their major, but timing is an important consideration. As I noted earlier, people in their early twenties, whose brains are still maturing, can be impulsive decision-makers who don't always stop and think about the consequences of their choices. Switching majors may seem like a good idea at the moment, but doing so as a sophomore is very different than doing so at the start of senior year.

Adam, who began school at a large public university, is floundering. He started his freshman year as a biology major, hoping to become a veterinarian. As the year progressed, he discovered that this career path required a lot of difficult and time-consuming science courses in which he performed poorly, and he abandoned his plan. He briefly considered many different areas of study, but he couldn't zero in on any one of them. His girlfriend, who was majoring in art history at a different college, suggested that Adam try her field, which she very much liked and hoped they could share.

Without giving it much thought, he changed all the science courses he had registered for in advance of his sophomore year to those required for an art history degree—only to discover at the end of his sophomore year that art history wasn't right for him. He decided to switch majors again, this time to business. Unfortunately, he hadn't looked closely at the business curriculum before making his decision. A degree in business required courses in calculus, statistics, and financial analysis—none of which he had taken in his first two years—as prerequisites for most other classes. If he wanted a degree in business, he essentially had to start school all over again. He stuck it out, but it took him a total of six and a half years to earn a bachelor's degree, and when he finished, he was just as ambivalent about having studied business as he had been about biology and art history.

Other students flounder scholastically *after* finishing college. They enroll in advanced-degree programs hoping to complete them, discover they've made a bad decision, and switch to an academic program in a different field either before or after completing the previous one. Here, too, there are differences between those who do this hastily and those who do it with a cogent plan.

Some students enter or change postcollege degree programs because they're responding to what they believe to be imminent changes in the labor force. They try to predict which economic sectors will be hiring two years later and ready themselves for the openings they're confident will proliferate. The problem is that these predictions aren't always accurate. If someone can reliably predict where the economy will be in two or three years, they'd be better off skipping further education and investing the money they'd spend on tuition in the companies they think will be leading the transformation. Dropping out of a program or starting a new one (or both) because of a hunch about the future is a bad idea.

There are, of course, all-purpose advanced degrees—like an MBA—that may be useful to those who haven't made up their mind about their career path. But these programs (at least the good ones) are hard to get into and very expensive, and they may not be worth the return on investment in comparison with taking an entry-level position in an industry and working one's way up the ladder in the same amount of time as the degree program takes.

If your child is considering an advanced degree to get a leg up when applying for a job, encourage them to consult with someone in their preferred field who can provide candid information about careers in that industry. Some may advise going back to school for the advanced degree; others may say it's not worth the money or time. The best route to success isn't always accumulating more letters after your name.

There's a very different type of perpetual student who just loves going to school, excels at it, and changes plans frequently but thoughtfully. I wouldn't call this floundering, but it can be frustrating for parents who worry about how long their kid is staying in school, and at what financial cost.

Take Amy, for example. After she earned her bachelor's degree in psychology in four years, she completed a two-year master's program in counseling, which got her thinking about going for a doctorate in clinical psychology. Following four years of classes and a doctoral dissertation, she completed the clinical internship required for licensure. During her internship year at a university hospital, she became friends with many medical school students and decided that what she really wanted was a career in medicine, perhaps specializing in neurology. But applying to medical school entailed completing a special postbaccalaureate program designed for students who as undergraduates hadn't taken the required science classes.

Always a high achiever who never found a class she didn't like, Amy sailed through this preparatory program in a year, attending daytime, evening, and summer classes. Ultimately, she got into an excellent med school—where she discovered the possibility of enrolling in a joint six-year program in medicine and law, leading to degrees in both. Amy couldn't resist—the intersection of law and neuroscience sounded so interesting. She knew that after finishing the program's coursework in medicine and law, she would need to complete a three-year medical residency followed by a neurology fellowship, but that didn't deter her. All told, Amy spent twenty years in training before she was done. She was close to forty before she started earning a salary, a lot of which she had to devote to paying off student loans. But she was thrilled with what she had accomplished and enjoyed every minute of it. And she ended up on faculty at a law school, teaching courses in law and neuroscience.

Parents should have very different reactions if Adam or Amy were their child. In Adam's case, they should consider the possibility that his indecisiveness might reflect some underlying psychological problem, like depression or anxiety. If his indecision about school was linked to more general difficulties in developing an accurate and positive view of himself and plans for the future, he might be struggling with what psychologists sometimes call "identity diffusion," a lack of a coherent sense of self, which some experts see as linked to ambivalence over becoming independent from one's parents.

Changing majors in college once or twice is common. But before your child attempts a third change of majors, encourage them to speak to someone at their college's student counseling center. I'd also encourage someone who changes majors and career plans frequently and impulsively to consider taking a gap year before switching majors yet again, doing something productive other than going to school. They can use the time away from college to think about what course of study and career they'd like to pursue without having to deal simultaneously with the day-to-day demands of going to school (see chapter 4, "Alternatives to Traditional College" on page 91).

Apart from the financial issues, there's little reason to be concerned about a young adult like Amy, whose decisions about continuing her education followed a logical sequence that reflected a lot of thought about what she wanted to do with her life. She's an ambitious young woman who loves learning new things—there's nothing wrong with that.

Parents with kids like Amy should check in with them from time to time just to make sure their mental and physical health are holding up. Maybe they're managing all of their schooling happily and successfully, without stress or regret. As long as they're content with their decision to postpone employment for the additional years of training—even if they accumulate a fair amount of student loan debt—I wouldn't be concerned. Twenty years of schooling and training seems like a very long time. But it's possible to start one's career at forty and do something one loves for four decades or more before retiring.

## Uncertainty About a Career

Some parents tell me that their child hasn't yet "found" themselves, which usually means they haven't settled into a career. Figuring out what you want to do in life is closely connected to developing a sense of identity, a deeper understanding of your values and goals, your strengths and weaknesses, than you had when you were a teenager. In modern society, the most common way to define ourselves is by our occupation. This is why parents worry about a child who is in their mid- or late twenties and still has no idea what they want to do with their life. It feels tantamount to saying they have no idea who they are.

As the world of work has changed, so has the process of deciding on a career. Today there are more options to choose among, and they change rapidly in their nature and availability. It's possible to make up your mind about a future occupation and go through the necessary training, only to find out that the job you were hoping to get doesn't really exist anymore, has changed dramatically since you began preparing for it, or is in such short supply that it might as well have disappeared.

This change in the nature of work has made it harder to tell whether a young person's career development is floundering. It takes people longer to figure out what they want to do with their lives nowadays because there are so many more options to choose among and those options are often more fleeting.

It's like the difference between shopping a few generations ago for milk—when your decision came down to whole milk, low-fat, or skim—versus today, where there are so many products to choose among: oat milk, soy milk, coconut milk, almond milk, non-GMO, and more. Today, a trip through the dairy aisle can be paralyzing. So can searching for a career.

Deciding on a career is largely about narrowing things down from the general to the specific, and floundering can occur at any of several phases in this process. You need to understand which phase your kid is in to determine whether and how best to help them.

The first phase is figuring out what you want from a job. According to experts in career development, there are seven basic kinds of rewards a job can provide: income, authority, creativity, altruism, stability, socializing, and leisure. One way to help a young adult who can't decide on a career is to ask which of these are most important. (If they say, "All of them," the right response is "Good luck with that!") This exercise is a good place to start because knowledge about specific occupations isn't necessary to answer the question. By the time your child is in their twenties, they should have a rough idea of what they're hoping to get from a job. If they're having trouble doing this, there are different types of tests—called "occupational interest inventories"—that ask dozens of questions and analyze someone's answers in a way that helps identify their priorities. Many such questionnaires are available online, usually for a modest fee.

The second phase involves identifying a field in which one's most important values are likely to be satisfied. For example, many different fields provide chances to be altruistic—to help others—among them, teaching, medicine, counseling, social work, and philanthropy. Similarly, lots of fields allow for creativity, including visual arts, performing arts, writing, engineering, and architecture. Sometime during the last year or so of college, people develop a rough idea about how they might realize their hopes for a gratifying career, often as a result of classes they've enjoyed and done well in. If your child is having trouble at this point, ask them to think about the courses they liked and explain what they liked about them. Colleges also provide occupational counseling, where your child can schedule an interview with someone who's trained to help students who are having trouble deciding on a career.

The third phase narrows things down to specific occupations within a general field. This often requires a level of knowledge that people outside the field don't have, so the extent to which a parent can help here depends on their own expertise and experience. Your child may want to go into law, engineering, or banking but doesn't yet know the subspecialties within the field. If your own work isn't associated with the field that interests your child, you won't know much more than they do. If they're floundering at this point, encouraging them to look at university course catalogs, which are widely available online, can be helpful, even if they're not interested in going for an advanced degree. Scrolling through course offerings might enable them to see the range of subspecialties in the discipline.

As we've already seen, one of the biggest recent changes in the world of work is the increased amount of training needed for an entry-level job. Many jobs that might have been available to a high school graduate thirty years ago now require some college, or even a college degree. A job that required a college degree in the past may now require training beyond college. Opportunities to learn very specific skills that hadn't been acquired in college, like "boot camps" in computer coding, are helpful and well worth the expense if your child is certain that a job they're interested in requires the knowledge such programs offer. They rarely provide financial aid, however, although every so often some sort of scholarship, loan, or payment plan is available.

Some people think that in today's workplace, *any* relevant additions to one's training beyond a bachelor's degree give an applicant an advantage. Some of the educational extras people feel forced to acquire today may increase job prospects because they genuinely are important for success in a particular occupation, some may influence hiring decisions because they reflect well on an applicant's character and perseverance, and others may reflect little more than a sort of "inflation," where over time, entry requirements have just drifted upward (just like college GPAs). Inflation may justify your cynicism about these requirements, but don't overlook them completely. Your child may genuinely have to spend time in postcollege education or training if it's the price of admission to a good job.

More generic "institutes" or one-off courses, in which attendees are exposed over a couple of sessions to the tricks of the trade in an industry through "immersive" experiences and guest presentations by well-known professionals, are probably not worth the investment—which can be substantial—if your child's hope is that they'll open doors for them. These programs may be informative, but they're unlikely to enhance an applicant's qualifications or appeal to someone reading their resume.

If your child has a specific career in mind but is having difficulty finding suitable job openings, getting interviews, or receiving actual offers, suggest that they think about working as an unpaid intern, perhaps with some temporary financial help from you, while they continue their search. This may be a better way to acquire relevant skills, learn about an industry's inner workings, and make contacts that might lead to a paid position than paying to enroll in an "institute." Your child's college probably has a student employment services office that can be helpful in finding internship leads, and many offices make these services available to alums as well as current students.

Internships don't always lead to full-time jobs, but they can put someone in the right place at the right time, as William, a recent liberal arts graduate, discovered.

During his sophomore year at Tulane, William decided to major in English, with the hope of someday going into publishing. After graduation he moved to New York, the home of all the country's major publishers, and began his job search. He soon discovered that publishing is a very popular field among recent graduates who majored in English, and entry-level jobs are hard to come by.

William remembered that his college roommate's mother worked in publishing, and he got her contact information from his buddy and reached out for advice. She suggested he come to her office to meet with her in person. During their meeting, she told him she didn't know of any openings in her department and asked if he'd be willing to work as an unpaid intern while he waited for a paid position to open up. She made a few calls and found that a colleague in the sales department would be happy to speak with him.

Although sales wasn't the aspect of publishing that interested him—most English graduates interested in publishing aspire to become editors—William was happy to have a foot in the door. By day, he worked on spreadsheets that tracked orders for titles on the publisher's backlist. In the evening, he sent out query letters to publishing houses and searched their websites for job openings.

One advantage of doing an internship, as opposed to attending an institute, is that an internship gets you physically into the setting where you'd like to work. One morning, on the way up from the lobby to his cubicle, William struck up a conversation with another passenger in the elevator. She introduced herself and asked what he did.

"Right now, I'm doing an internship in the sales department," he explained. "But I hope to eventually get into editorial."

"You know," the woman said, "I think one of the editors on our team is looking for an editorial assistant. You ought to apply." Being an editorial assistant is the first rung on a long ladder up to becoming an editor, but it's the way most young people interested in editing start. She handed William her card and asked him to email her so she could get back to him with the editor's contact information. He thanked her as he stepped off the elevator and promised to follow up. When the doors closed behind him he looked at the woman's card. She was one of the publisher's vice presidents.

The moment William got to his desk, he sent an email once again thanking her for the tip. She replied later that day with the name of the editor, confirming that he would be hiring an assistant. William wrote to the editor, relaying his elevator conversation and expressing his interest in the job. He attached a copy of his resume.

That evening, he got an email from the editor asking if he could come in for an interview the following morning. "Always happy to meet a fellow Tulane grad!" he had written. "And especially someone who responds quickly—that's essential in this business." He didn't tell William his assistant had quit two days before to take a better job at another publisher, and that he needed to replace her in a hurry.

William stayed up that night and searched the internet for the titles of books the editor had worked on. He read summaries of many of them and was able to impress the editor during their meeting with his knowledge about his portfolio. Three days later, after a few other candidates had been interviewed, William was offered the job. He was initially assigned clerical work—managing the editor's calendar, responding to routine email, and so on. But he also got to attend many meetings during which he learned a lot about the industry from the inside. After his first year, he was given a modest raise and promoted to assistant editor, which is the next rung up the editorial career ladder. He got a taste of what it's like to deal with authors (sometimes wonderful, sometimes frustrating, he discovered). And he was glad he'd been willing to do the internship.

❧

It takes longer to settle into a career nowadays, but settling in isn't the same as floundering. There's a difference between accumulating additional training with a goal and plan in mind, which makes sense in today's labor force, and haphazardly bouncing around between unrelated jobs or training programs. That's not planning; that's floundering. Working in a non-career-related job, like busing tables or tending bar, to support yourself while figuring out what to do with your life is fine as long as the work part leaves adequate time and energy for the figuring-out part.

Parents may understand all this in principle but nevertheless watch their child accumulate a lot of postcollege training or work in a series of dead-end jobs and wonder when "enough is enough." Unless you're in the field your child is interested in, or have knowledgeable friends, relatives, or colleagues your child might call, I don't think there's any way of knowing how much time it usually takes for someone to break into a field. A lot depends on the current state of hiring in a given industry. Some occupations, like acting, are infamous for how long it takes to get one's first job, much less steady employment. In other occupations, like computer engineering, qualified applicants may get job offers in no time at all.

Many parents also wonder whether a child in their late twenties or thirties is floundering because they're considering changing careers, perhaps for a second or third time. Before reaching a conclusion about this, remember that the typical pattern of career development has changed greatly in recent generations. The old model of careers, in which a person's first job often determined the path they followed for life, has been replaced by one in which multiple job or career changes over one's lifetime is the norm.

People change careers for all sorts of reasons, some sensible and some questionable. If your child is considering a change, and they've thought it out, done their homework, are financially secure, and have genuine opportunities to explore, you should support their decision. Perhaps they're contemplating something they'd always wanted to do but never prepared for, and their finances are now sound enough to return to school to retrain. This approach is more common than you might realize. More than a quarter of American undergraduates today are twenty-five or older, and one in every ten college students is at least thirty-five, and these numbers don't even count older students enrolled in graduate and professional schools.

Because we're living so much longer today than a generation ago (notwithstanding the recent and hopefully temporary decline in life expectancy due to COVID), it makes perfect sense for people to have multiple careers. Maybe by the time your child is approaching forty they've enjoyed what they've been doing but want a new set of challenges. Maybe they began their work life in a career they've always seen as a way station, an occupational placeholder until they figured out what they really wanted to do. Or perhaps after giving it a lot of thought and working for a half-dozen years, they realized that their current job is making them unhappy. If their work is making them irritable, stressed out, or depressed, and has been for a while, it may be time to move on. Besides the impact their situation is taking on their own mental health, their foul mood may be making life difficult for their partner or children.

If your child is contemplating changing careers, they may or may not want to discuss it with you. You should withhold any negative opinions you have about any tentative decisions they've mentioned unless they're thinking of quitting a job without having a new one lined up, are in a tenuous financial situation, or are impulsive by nature, in which case you might gently ask about how long they'll be able to survive without a salary. This may worry you, but for all you know, they may have an emergency fund that they've saved for precisely this purpose. If their decision seems especially impulsive, ask whether they've considered the possibility of losing certain benefits, which is why many people stay in jobs they're not wholly satisfied with. Quitting in a huff can threaten their health insurance.

If you think your child's decision has been carefully considered, you can certainly pose a few questions to show your interest in this aspect of their life, but resist offering opinions unless you're asked for them. You may not have made the same change if you were in their shoes, but their shoes may be a bad fit for you. This is their choice to make, whether you approve or not. Here's another instance where the best course is to follow the maxim I introduced earlier: *Speak up when you must, but unless your child specifically asks for it, keep your opinion to yourself.*

It's far better to leave a job you're miserable in than spend a lifetime in a career you abhor. This is something many people in previous generations did because career changes were difficult to make and frowned upon. It's great that this stigma is a thing of the past, especially since people nowadays work well into their seventies before retiring. That's a long time to be unhappy about such a big part of your life.

Perhaps your child's career is on track and you're more concerned about their love life—or lack thereof. As with their progress in the world of work, you need to look at how their love life is developing in the context of social changes that have altered the timetable of adult development.

## Still Single (After All These Years)

Melanie had been suffering from insomnia on and off for about six years, ever since her husband died in his early fifties from a sudden heart attack. At the time, her doctor assured her that it was common for recently widowed people to have problems sleeping and prescribed a mild sedative to take before bed each night.

After three years of using the medicine—which indeed helped her fall asleep—and after hearing so many news stories about people becoming addicted to prescription medication, she gradually withdrew herself from the drug. She was able to sleep again without taking her bedtime pill. But about two years later, her insomnia returned. It had nothing to do with her husband's death, though. She couldn't stop worrying about her thirty-three-year-old daughter, Laurie, who wasn't engaged or married, unlike most of her friends from college. She wasn't even living with someone. Nor did she appear to have any prospects.

The thought that her daughter would spend her life unmarried saddened Melanie. She'd enjoyed a happy marriage for nearly twenty-five years, and she knew how lonely it can be to live alone. And, selfishly, she was hoping that Laurie would marry and start a family, so that she'd have grandchildren to help fill, at least partly, the hole that Charlie's death had left in her heart.

As she tossed and turned each night, wondering whether she should call her doctor and ask for a refill of her sleep medication, Melanie would run through a mental list of Laurie's assets—she was pretty, smart, successful, and fun, often described by her friends as the life of the party. She was just too picky about the men she dated, Melanie thought.

Whenever Melanie would ask about her "nightlife" (which her

daughter knew was a not-so-subtle way of asking if she'd met anyone she was interested in), Laurie explained that she had a satisfying social life but still hadn't found the right person. But surely there was someone out there, Melanie would say to herself—there had to be in a city the size of Seattle—who would be attracted to her daughter and attractive enough for her daughter to get serious about.

Many parents of unmarried children in their late thirties have similar concerns. If you do, too, perhaps knowing a little about the current state of marriage in America will allay them.

❧

Like many aspects of the transition to adulthood, the age at which people first marry has been getting progressively older. In 2021, the average age of a first marriage among American women was twenty-eight; among men, it was around thirty. A generation before, in 1991, the average American woman got married when she was twenty-four, whereas the average age among men was twenty-six. A generation before that, in 1961, these ages were twenty and twenty-three, respectively. No other transition into adulthood has been delayed by nearly this much. The remarkable increase over the last half century has occurred across the socioeconomic spectrum.

Social class may not affect *when* people marry, but it's an important influence on *whether* they do. Although marriage rates in the U.S. have been declining overall, the extent of that decline varies tremendously by social class. Marriage is far less common nowadays among poor and working-class people than in the past, when the majority of people from all walks of life married, as was the case in the 1970s. But plenty of people still get married. According to recent estimates, close to 80 percent of people in the top 40 percent of the U.S. income distribution (those with annual household incomes exceeding $100,000) are married, pretty much the same proportion as it was *forty years before.*

Plus, alarmist reports on the demise of marriage in America don't mention the 15 percent of nonmarried people between the ages of twenty-five and thirty-four who are living with a partner, two-thirds of whom say they plan to marry once they find their financial footing. Nor do they include the 60 percent of people who've never married, but who say they hope to get hitched one day. And, then, of course, there are many divorced people who hope to remarry. Marriage is by no means disappearing, but it is undeniably being delayed.

However, cohabitation has become an enduring way of life in many poorer segments of the population (families whose income is below the fiftieth percentile), which is why their marriage rate is so low. On the other hand, for lots of more affluent couples, cohabitation is a temporary state that precedes marriage. Today, more than 75 percent of all first marriages in the United States are preceded by some period of cohabitation. If your child is living with their partner, but not legally married, you shouldn't be concerned about their well-being. Cohabitation has become increasingly accepted in American society. And, in case you've wondered, there's no evidence that a couple's likelihood of divorcing is affected, one way or the other, by whether they lived together before getting married. Although many people think of cohabitation as a trial run that protects against a subsequent divorce, it's not.

As with other markers of adulthood, it's misleading to judge your child's marital "progress" by the timetable you followed when you were their age. If you factor in the large numbers of young people who are cohabitating with someone in a relationship that's a marriage in all but the legal sense, today's romantic timetable isn't all that different than it was when you were a young adult.

Today, well over half of all women between the ages of twenty-five and twenty-nine, and more than two-thirds of men this age, have never been married. Among people between thirty and thirty-four, about one-third of women and more than 40 percent of men have never been married. Even among those between thirty-five and thirty-nine, more than one-fifth of women and more than one-fourth of men have never been part of a married couple. These numbers don't include unmarried couples who live together, so they overestimate the proportion of young people who are romantically unattached.

My point is that if your child is in their thirties—even their late thirties—and still single, and you're desperately hoping that they'll marry someday, there's no reason to panic. Nearly one-third of all unmarried people in their late thirties get married before they're forty-five, and nearly half get married before they're fifty.

Some parents are especially concerned about missing out on grandparenting if their child remains unattached into their late thirties. Statistically speaking, this is more of an issue if your child is a daughter than a son. There's a substantial drop in women's fertility after age thirty-five, and especially after age forty, and this is true even among those who try to conceive using IVF. For example, IVF is successful half the time among women under thirty-five, but less than 5 percent of the time among those who are forty-two and older. Keep in mind, though, that IVF success rates among women in their forties have been improving, and physicians can now assess a couple's likelihood of having a successful IVF based on numerous hormonal markers that can be measured before they start trying to conceive. Men's fertility also declines with age, but the main drop occurs later for them—around age forty—than it does for women. As is the case among women, the drop in male fertility after age forty also affects a couple's likelihood of successful IVF.

☙

If you're unhappy that your grown child is unattached, the most important thing to think about is *their* psychological state, not yours. Some people are perfectly happy being single—indeed, a growing number of people say they prefer to be single—so don't assume that just because you're unhappy about your kid's situation, they're unhappy, too.

The same goes for whether you'll get to be a grandparent someday. You may fantasize about having a grandchild, but don't conflate your hopes with your child's wishes. Besides, many single people in their twenties who proclaim they never want to have kids change their mind later, and a growing number of people have or adopt children without getting married.

This caution applies regardless of whether your child is in a relationship or single. Just because someone is married doesn't mean they want to be a parent. Recent surveys show that more than a third of adults under the age of forty who don't have children plan on remaining childless, and well over half of them say the reason is that they just don't want to be parents (the rest say that they have other priorities, financial worries, or health problems). If you have a sibling, perhaps you can satisfy some of your wishes for a grandchild by being an unusually involved aunt or uncle, or by taking a special interest in a friend's children. Children often benefit from relationships with adults who aren't their parents or grandparents, and during adolescence, in particular, may prefer the company of nonfamily adults.

If your child is unattached and has told you they wish they weren't, it's best to empathize, but keep your own disappointment or worry about this to yourself. I doubt there are many young people these days who get married just to please their parents, and the last thing you want is to pressure your child into getting into a relationship for *your* benefit. If it appears that they are floundering romantically—a long sequence of short-lived relationships that start out well but end badly or unexpectedly—and you've felt comfortable discussing their romantic life with them in the past, ask them for their take on what's been happening. You might suggest talking to a therapist if they are baffled, upset, or depressed by the situation. In my experience, psychotherapy is often effective in helping people understand and correct maladaptive patterns in the way they choose or interact with prospective partners.

If you know of someone your child might enjoy dating, it's fine to let your child know, so long as you base your opinion on what type of person your child is likely to be attracted to rather than the sort of person you wish they were attracted to, or just because you think they'd be happier if they were married—that their being with *anyone* is better than remaining single. In the past, people got married for all sorts of reasons that had nothing to do with love. That's no longer the case in America, where 90 percent of married people say that being in love was the main reason for marrying their partner. Only around a third said that an important reason was to have children, and just 10 percent mentioned finances or convenience.

Avoid making suggestions about how to find that special someone. Your child knows a lot more about this than you. It's a different dating world out there than when you were young and single.

## When Your Child Moves Back Home

A final source of worry about a young adult who seems to be floundering can arise after an adult child has moved back home. For many parents, this is a major source of worry, in part because few people in their generation did and in part because living so close to your child gives you a ringside seat to their life. It's easier for a parent to remain in the dark about their child's educational, occupational, and romantic prospects, as well as their mental health, when they aren't living under the same roof. When an adult child moves back home, though, familiarity can breed anxiety.

When an adult child moves back home with you, it raises different issues than those that arise when college students come home during scheduled breaks of a week or two, or even for a couple of months during the summer. These breaks sometimes put a strain on family relationships (see chapter 4, "Visits Home from College" on page 96), but because they're time-limited, all concerned are more likely to see any disagreements as temporary—and therefore endurable—irritations.

Here, I focus on moves back home that will last for some indeterminate period of time, typically because the child can't afford to live anywhere else. These relocations have been happening more frequently over the past several decades. More young adults now live with their parents than at any time since the beginning of the twentieth century. In the United States, this is now the most common living arrangement among people between the ages of eighteen and twenty-nine.

As of 2020, more than half of American young people between eighteen and twenty-nine were living with one or both parents, surpassing the percentage even at the height of the Great Depression. The proportion has risen from 30 percent in 1960 to just over 50 percent today. So if your child needs to move back home, you're not alone—and your child is not an anomaly to worry about.

The latest increase in the proportion of young people who live with one or both parents might be chalked up to the pandemic, but the trend was in place well before. There was a steep increase in the percentage of young adults living with one or both parents between 2005 and early 2020, before the pandemic was even recognized, likely because of the Great Recession, which took a disproportionate toll on young adults. The trend has been more or less universal: living with one's parents has become more common among both males and females, across all ethnic groups, in both metropolitan and rural areas, and in different parts of the country.

The biggest increase in young adults living at home since 2020 has been among those who are under twenty-five, because this age group has been the most likely to lose their jobs or take pay cuts. Moving back in with their parents was necessary for economic survival. But the phenomenon has by no means been limited to this age group. In early 2020, more than one-quarter of people between the ages of twenty-five and twenty-nine were living with one or both parents. This figure has not declined in the past few years.

❧

The psychological contexts of a visit home from college and moving back in with one or both parents couldn't be more different. The first provides a chance for your child to show you how grown up they've become. They have tasted independence in college, and they like the taste. As we've seen, most disagreements that arise during these visits involve issues where the young person thinks they aren't being treated like the adult they now think they are (see chapter 4, "Visits Home from College" on page 96).

Moving back in with their parents can feel just the opposite to your kid. When anyone who's been living on their own is forced to move back home, they feel less like a fully independent adult. A visit home from college often feels like a vacation; moving back in often feels like a warning sign.

Regardless of whether the reasons for your child's return were beyond their control—say, their company folded or had to lay off workers—it feels to them like a step backward. This may be an inaccurate impression, but in many cases it's unavoidable. In addition, moving back home is usually an indeterminate arrangement. Unlike a break from school, it doesn't end when the college calendar dictates it. It ends when your child gets back on their feet—when they can once again afford to feed and house themselves. No one knows for sure when this will happen. This uncertainty can create a lot of anxiety for everyone, because no one wants the arrangement to continue any longer than necessary, but no one wants to end it prematurely. Few people do well when they're living with ambiguity.

The psychological impact of moving back in with one's parents is also more fraught in a society like ours, in which doing so hasn't been the norm historically, as it is in other cultures. Americans place a premium on independence as a measure of adulthood. In many other countries, though, being happily "interdependent" is viewed as the true mark of maturity. In many Asian cultures, in particular, viewing oneself as independent from one's parents is seen as an immature unwillingness to grow up. And in some European countries, like Italy, it's normal for young adults to live with their parents until they themselves are married, or even beyond if finances require it or if their family expects it. No Italian would denigrate a young person for living at home after college, and we shouldn't, either.

Returning home doesn't signal that your child has failed or that you've been unsuccessful as a parent. But you should be careful not to do or say anything that could make them feel they haven't lived up to society's standards. Parents should treat a grown child who's moved back home as a competent and capable adult. In order to do this, you need to reincorporate your child into your family as a full-fledged adult member of the household without creating the impression that this is some sort of regression, or something that might become permanent. There are three ways to do this.

The first, and most important, is to have an honest conversation about your expectations of each other. The concerns parents might discuss with college students about how they should behave when they're home should not be brought up once an older child has moved back. In fact, discussing these topics only makes your child feel less mature, as if they're reliving their high school years with you.

Think about it this way: If your thirty-five-year-old sister fell on hard times and needed to live with you for a while, you wouldn't talk with her about what time she needed to be home at night, the importance of keeping her bedroom tidy, or the need to keep you apprised of her whereabouts. There's no need to discuss these matters with an adult child who's moved back home, either. Be especially careful not to fall back into familiar dynamics that were in place the last time your child lived with you full-time, probably when they were a teenager. You may have not changed a lot since then, but they certainly have.

Second, it's essential that your child contribute to the household, not necessarily financially (especially if they have moved back in because they're low on funds), but by pitching in with day-to-day activities. They should help with cooking, cleaning, shopping, doing laundry, shoveling snow, and so forth—and any major projects, like home repairs or renovations, either by themselves or jointly with you.

Don't ask them to just take care of themselves and leave everything else for you to do—that they're responsible for doing their own laundry but no one else's, or that they have a section of the refrigerator designated as theirs, or that they clean their bedroom but not common spaces like the kitchen or family room. They're not guests at a bed-and-breakfast, and you shouldn't treat them that way.

Some parents expect children who move back home to pay something for room and board, but if the ultimate goal is to help your child get back on their financial feet, this is counterproductive. It will only prolong their need to live with you. If they're employed, they should be saving their earnings until they can again afford living on their own. If they are working but have trouble saving a lot of their pay, make a plan together to have them contribute something for rent that's deposited into a savings account until they move out. They can use this nest egg to get back on their feet instead of asking you for help.

Finally, you should have an explicit mutual understanding about how your child will spend their days. If they're still in school, they should be taking classes, working on assignments, and studying for exams—just as they would be doing if they lived on their own—and they'll need a quiet place to do their schoolwork. You don't need to monitor them, any more than you would monitor their scholastic activities if they weren't living with you (see chapter 4, "Appropriate Involvement in Your Child's College Education" on page 86). If they have a job, they should behave just as they would if they weren't living at home, and you shouldn't monitor their activities, like what time they leave for work or whether they work at home in the evenings or on weekends.

If your child needs a job, they should be taking steps to land one. This can include enrolling in classes that will make them more competitive on the job market, searching job listings and posting their resume online, networking with acquaintances who may be able to assist them, and going on job interviews. If they want to work at a job that isn't career-related just to earn money, this is fine as long as they're saving their earnings and also doing things that could lead to a position in the field they're interested in.

Deciding how to respond if your kid refuses to abide by the rules you've agreed on is tricky. There are two categories of violations, each meriting a different response. The first involves shared household responsibilities that your kid refuses or forgets to fulfill. The second concerns activities aimed at accumulating the resources necessary to allow moving out (assuming that this is the goal), like a job, an advanced degree, or enough savings to pay for their own place to live.

With respect to the first, I've cautioned against falling back into the dynamics that characterized your relationship when your child was a teenager, before they left home for college. This will take its toll on your mental health (because squabbling over mundane things, like undone chores, missed appointments, or empty bags of chips left on the coffee table, will be just as annoying to you now as they were ten years ago, if not more so) and your kid's (because being nagged by your parents is unpleasant no matter how old you are). It's not going to work to treat your adult child like a teenager just because they've starting acting like their adolescent self.

In this case, sit down with your kid and engage in "collaborative problem-solving" (see chapter 2, "Resolving Disputes Constructively" on page 40). As a reminder, this process involves the two of you discussing the problem, brainstorming possible solutions to it, making a tentative plan to solve it, and after some time (like a couple of weeks) evaluating whether it's working. Moving the laundry basket out of their bedroom closet and into the corner of their bedroom will get them to take care of it when they see clothes overflowing. Attaching a grocery list to the refrigerator door will prompt them to add things to the list when something has run out. Leaving the snow shovel next to the front door the night before a large snowfall is predicted will remind them to clear the driveway before leaving the house in the morning. The key is to make sure that each of you is contributing to the solution and to figuring out how it might be tweaked to become more effective. If your kid continues to walk by the snow shovel on their way out, place the shovel so that it's impossible to open the door without picking it up. If nothing like this works, have a serious conversation about the problem, indicate that if things don't change they'll have to find somewhere else to live, and establish some sort of timetable for them to find a new place to live. You may not find it easy to loan them some money they can use to move out, but this could be easier on everyone than constant bickering. And if you can't subsidize them, you can assist them with finding employment. If your child has difficulty moving out because of a mental health problem or addiction, help them get appropriate treatment (see chapter 3, "Getting Help" on page 62).

As for helping to ensure that your kid is doing things that will help them get back the job or home they need, a combination of vigilance and patience is necessary. You need to monitor their activities without becoming a nag. It's fine to ask every once in a while how their job search is going, but this isn't something you should do multiple times each week. If the job market is tight, it will take time to find a decent job. Ask if there's anything you can do to help, but be sensitive to their response. "No thanks" may mean "I've got it under control," but it can also mean "Mind your own business." If you think they're saying the former, you can respond with "That's great, but if you ever need an extra pair of eyes, I'm happy to help." If they're saying the latter, you need to figure out whether they're doing what's reasonable and just not having any success (in which case they may be depressed or embarrassed about their lack of progress) or not trying hard enough. If it's the former, express sympathy and say, "Yes, it's not my business, but that doesn't mean I can't ask how things are going. I'm just being courteous and I expect the same in return." If it's the latter, say something like "When you first moved back, you said that you would spend all of your free time job hunting. If you're at a point where there aren't any prospects, we can find things for you to do to help out around here until the job market improves." If your kid refuses, it's time to jointly set a schedule for them moving out.

I've outlined how to handle problems with a kid who's moved back home. But it's pretty unlikely you'll have such problems. On national surveys, most young adults who've moved back home say that they and their parents get along fine. During the pandemic I taught several senior seminars remotely by Zoom, in which many of the twentysomethings in my classes had been forced to move back home and attend class from their childhood bedroom or the kitchen table. Most of them wished they were living on their own again, but just about all of them said that living with their parents had strengthened their relationship; helped them get to know their parents better as people, not just parents; and made them even more appreciative of everything their parents do and have done for them.

❧

Figuring out whether your kid is floundering is a challenge because many of the impediments to moving successfully into and through adulthood are out of their control, like overenrolled classes that make it impossible to get a degree in four years, a dearth of desirable people to date, an exceptionally tight job market, or sky-high housing prices. If your kid appears to be doing what seems reasonable without success, remember that things are different now than they were when you were their age. It takes young people longer to finish school, establish a career, start a family, and become economically dependent. As I've said before, "When I was your age" isn't the right way to think about your kid's circumstances. It takes more time to become an adult these days than it did a generation ago. And it requires more sympathy and patience from their parents.

## CHAPTER EIGHT

# Grandparenthood

## How to Help the New Parents

Grandparenting brings many of the same pleasures you had when you were raising your own child, without the challenging, often exhausting responsibilities that parents have. This leaves time and energy to create a relationship with your grandchild built largely around having fun together. If you aren't yet a grandparent, or have just become one, this is an excellent way to approach your new relationship. Leave the discipline to your child and their partner. Focus on cherishing your grandchild and enjoying your time together.

Being a good grandparent is important for your grandchild's well-being, their parents', and yours, too. Grandchildren who have a close relationship with a grandparent reap many psychological benefits. A baby forms attachments with people in addition to their parents, and every additional bond gives them more emotional security. Forming an attachment to you will positively influence your grandchild's cognitive, social, and emotional development beyond what they get out of their relationships with their parents.

As children grow, grandparents often do many of the same things that parents do, but with their own style and interests. When you read and play with your grandchildren and choose different books, toys, and activities than the children's parents, you expand and diversify their experiences. Take some time to think about the positive and enjoyable experiences you might add to your grandchild's life that complement, but don't duplicate, what their parents bring.

The benefits of a close connection between a grandparent and grandchild flow in both directions. A close connection with a grandchild will make you less susceptible to depression and loneliness, more satisfied with life, and happier. If you can see your grandchild often, you'll find they keep you more active and feeling younger. As they grow, progress through school, and involve themselves with pop culture, you'll learn lots of new things from them. Grandchildren can also be an additional source of closeness between you, your child, and your child's partner, because they give all of you pleasure and an unending supply of new things to talk about.

Of course, being a good grandparent will help your child and their partner greatly. If you live close by or vacation together, you can babysit. From time to time your child and their partner may come to you for advice on how to handle some aspect of parenting, which I'll discuss later in this chapter. And regardless of where you live, depending on your finances, you might be able to defray some of the considerable expenses of outfitting a nursery or help pay for childcare.

❧

Later in this chapter, I'll discuss how to build a close relationship with your grandchild, but initially, being a good grandparent mainly involves making life easier for your child and their partner. Your help will be useful when the child is a bit older, too, but once a child enters preschool, spends less time at home, and is a little more self-sufficient, parenting becomes a lot easier.

Here are some guidelines for how to help when your grandchild is still an infant (two years and under):

*If you'd like to purchase a piece of equipment or furniture for your child and their partner, buy what they say they need, even if it's not what you were hoping to get them.* Suppose the parents-to-be are looking at a list of expensive equipment they need to purchase: a crib, a car seat, a stroller, furniture for the baby's room. You are planning on helping them. If you haven't researched the prices of these items, check them out before you make an offer, and prepare yourself for sticker shock. Numerous changes in the design and safety features of baby products have made them much more expensive than when you were a new parent.

Say you decide to help with a stroller and they have their eyes on a particular stroller that isn't the one you would choose. If they ask for your opinion or your help in selecting among several alternatives, speak up. But if they've told you which stroller they want, that's the one you should buy. If it's more than you planned to spend, give them the amount of money you had in mind to put toward the purchase. Yes, you were hoping to someday push the baby in a stroller you picked out, but your grandchild's parents are the ones who'll be using it every day.

*When the baby is born, give your child and their partner time at home with their newborn before you visit.* Ask the new parents what would be helpful. If you want to visit the hospital right after the birth, make sure it's okay with the new parents before popping in with an armful of balloons. And bear in mind that after they return home, many couples want some time alone to bond with the baby and form their own family unit.

The new parents' desire to be alone with their newborn isn't meant to exclude you, so don't take it that way. Nor is it a sign of how they'll treat you in the future. They're just as eager to have you meet their baby as you are to meet your grandchild. Just give them a little time to adapt to parenthood and to share their private thoughts and emotions with each other.

If this is their first child, the couple may be nervous or unsure about how to take care of an infant and aren't ready yet to do it in front of an audience. And sometimes it takes a mom more than a few days after leaving the hospital to recover physically and emotionally from childbirth, especially if it was a difficult labor, the delivery required a C-section, or she is suffering from mild, short-term postpartum depression (sometimes called the "baby blues"), which is reported by more than 70 percent of new mothers a few days after their delivery. Ask your child when it's okay to visit, respect the couple's wishes, and unless they request otherwise, keep your visits short at the beginning. You've probably forgotten how tiring it is to be a new parent.

*If you live nearby, offer to babysit without being asked.* A standing babysitting appointment after work every Thursday to allow an hour of child-free grocery shopping is helpful. A surprise or planned night out to have an adults-only dinner or see a movie without having to pay for a babysitter is a huge treat, especially if money is tight, as it often is for new parents. If you live far away but see your child's family for extended visits, make the same offer at least once while you're staying with them. They just might invite you to visit more often!

*Keep in mind that babysitting an infant or toddler is physically demanding.* You may be surprised at how hard it is to keep up with a baby who's crawling or constantly grabbing for things they shouldn't touch, or how heavy twenty pounds is when you have to bend over to pick the baby up or lift them out of their crib. Don't be shy about saying something if you discover you can't babysit for long stretches of time, and ask if the parents have an alternative who can cover part of your shift. Or ask a friend or relative to accompany you. It's dangerous for both you and the infant for you to babysit for hours when you can't manage it by yourself. It's easy for someone who isn't strong enough to repeatedly lift a baby to lose their balance and fall.

*If you can afford to, establish a college fund for your grandchild.* College is expensive now. We can only imagine how astronomical it will be when your grandchild turns eighteen. Even small amounts deposited periodically into a college savings account will grow over time into something sizable, especially if you begin contributing to it early in your grandchild's life. Don't, however, invest in a college fund to the detriment of your own living expenses and retirement.

There are different types of education savings accounts that allow your grandchild to later use the money for college expenses without having to pay taxes on what's withdrawn. These funds can also be used to pay for your grandchild's K–12 tuition (if they're not going to public school), and your grandchild can also use them later to repay student loans. The account remains under your control, so you don't have to worry about the money being misused. You can find information about these accounts online; programs vary from state to state.

*Indulge your grandchild from time to time, but don't violate any rules their parents have set.* If you know your child and their partner don't want their child to eat sugary foods, and the child is spending the night with you, don't pour them a bowl of sweet cereal for breakfast the next morning. If your grandchild looks at the cereal box and says, "My parents don't let me eat this kind of cereal because it has too much sugar," don't smile and explain that it will be your little secret.

If your grandchild knows what they're not allowed to eat, and if you feed your grandchild those foods, you're teaching them it's fine to disobey their parents. If that bowl of cereal is something you want to treat your grandchild to, ask their parents' permission out of the child's earshot. If they grant it, tell your grandchild when you serve breakfast that their parents told you it was okay this time.

*If you give your grandchild a present, make sure it's acceptable to their parents.* Parents often have policies about the playthings their children are allowed to have. Many don't permit toy guns, for example, and some don't allow electronic devices with screens before their child is a certain age. Abide by the parents' wishes. You don't want to watch your grandchild open your present only to be told by their parents that they can't keep it. If your gift is something your grandchild might already own, or if you have no idea what to buy, ask their parents. You may think it's fun to surprise parents with what you give their child, but no surprise is worth the prospect of disappointing your grandchild.

‫‬⁂

If your grandchild has other grandparents (or step-grandparents) in their life, you should be happy. A child can't have too many adults who love them. There's no reason to be jealous of your grandchild's relationships with other grandparents. Children have an unlimited capacity for close relationships with others, and your grandchild's love for other people does not subtract from their affection for you.

Actually, it's just the opposite—the more healthy attachments a child has, the easier they find it to be close to others.

If you hit it off with the other grandparents, that's an added bonus which makes it easier to bring the entire extended family together for holidays and the like. But whether you enjoy their company or not, their ideas about grandparenting may differ from yours. If that's the case, don't say or do anything. Leave their behavior to your child and their partner to worry about. However, if you think the other grandparents have been behaving in a way that has the potential to seriously harm your grandchild's well-being—you learn that they've been grossly negligent while babysitting, for example—voice your concerns to your child and their partner. The couple may not be aware of what the other grandparents have done (or failed to do). Make sure to be specific about what worries you.

And please don't compete with the other grandparents for your grandchild's affection or their parents' gratitude. You aren't in a contest to see who's the favorite. Just be the best grandparent *you* can be.

## Giving Advice About Your Child's Parenting

When Valerie and her husband, Paul, climbed into bed at the end of the first night of their visit, they lay on their backs for a while, holding hands without speaking. They were in the guest room, down the hall from their son and daughter-in-law's bedroom, and they were nervous about being overheard. Paul and his son, Drew, had gone to bed a little angry at each other.

"You really shouldn't have said anything," Valerie whispered.

"I couldn't help it."

"Well, Drew was angry about it."

"It was a total overreaction. I thought he was being rigid. All

I said was to relax a bit. Jillian wasn't sleepy. She asked to stay up longer as a special favor because we were visiting. Why couldn't she stay up another hour? We don't get to see her that often."

"It's a school night. She needs to get up tomorrow morning by seven."

"Oh, right. And she can't come to school late, I guess. She might miss a crucial lesson in finger painting."

"It's not that, dear. Drew said it would throw her whole sleep cycle off. She needs to wake up at the same time every day. My friend, Nina, says her daughter-in-law does the same thing with her four-year-old and that this is what all the books recommend."

"It sounds crazy to me," Paul said. "And, what, we can't give them a little friendly advice every once in a while? Isn't that what grandparents are for? Are we supposed to keep our mouths shut when we disagree with them?"

"Yes, we should. I read somewhere that grandparents should be seen and not heard."

"I think you've got that expression wrong—it's *children* who are supposed to be seen and not heard."

"Apparently, *that* advice has been thrown out the window. Didn't you notice that Jillian never stops interrupting? They really need to teach her some manners."

"Well, just don't say that in front of Drew. I don't know if their doghouse is big enough for both of us."

❧

If your child or their partner has done, or is about to do, something that could injure their child, you should certainly intervene. Speak up if you notice an electrical outlet they forgot to babyproof, if their baby has gotten ahold of a small object that could be a choking hazard, or if you see them lose their temper and spank or scream at their toddler when she throws a tantrum. Research now shows that spanking is harmful to children's development, and there are more effective ways to respond to a misbehaving three-year-old that will lessen the likelihood of tantrums in the future, like staying calm and distracting them.

But when it comes to the daily challenges of parenting, it's better to keep your opinions to yourself for three reasons.

First, fads and fashions in parenting change generationally. Today's parents have been advised to keep their babies on strict schedules for feeding and sleeping. Parents may use apps on their smartphones to remind them when it's time for a meal or a nap, and they might track these routines religiously, recording exact amounts of breast milk or formula consumed at each feeding and carefully monitoring the minutes clocked during each nap. It might strike you as a bit compulsive, but if you check out the most popular books for today's parents, this is the recommended approach. Like so much of life, raising children has become data-driven. Your child and their partner are behaving just like other parents their age.

Your generation was much more laid-back as parents. Dr. Spock's *Baby and Child Care*, which so many of us used as a parenting bible, encouraged parents to attend to their child's needs, rely on common sense, and adapt their parenting to their children's cues, rather than forcing infants to adjust their behavior to their parents' demands. Indeed, the first sentence in his classic book is "Trust yourself."

So you fed your baby when they seemed hungry and didn't track their daily food intake. You put them down for naps when they looked tired and waited for them to rouse naturally before getting them out of the crib. If you look at the advice books your generation relied on, you'll see that this was the guidance they were given. Today's new parents would be appalled at how laxly they were raised.

The funny thing, at least to someone like me who studies parenting and child development, is that it really doesn't matter which approach you follow. There are lots of ways to be a good parent and raise a healthy child.

Each generation thinks they've made a breakthrough discovery about how best to raise children. Most of the time, though, the hot "new" parenting techniques had been popular at some point in the past. Today's strict feeding and sleeping schedules were strongly recommended during the first half of the twentieth century—the approach was referred to as "scientific parenting." That style went out of fashion in the late 1940s, with Dr. Spock, who is about as antithetical to a rigid, preplanned, data-driven schedule as I can imagine. Today's version of Spock's book would probably start with "Trust the data."

When a grandparent who trusted themselves to follow their own baby's leads and allow them to direct their own feeding and sleeping regimens sees their child keeping their infant to a strict schedule, it's understandable that the grandparent wants to say something. And it won't be surprising if another generational difference of opinion surfaces thirty years from now, when today's parents chide their adult children for failing to keep their newborn on a schedule. The next generation of parenting gurus might very well advise flexibility when it comes to sleeping and feeding, and pitch a child-directed approach as another breakthrough, all the while disparaging the previous generation's data-driven parenting.

Your grandchild will turn out just fine whether they're on a tight schedule or none at all. Infant development is under strong, preprogrammed genetic control. It's a piece of inborn "software" that has worked well for thousands of years, regardless of the advice du jour. Humans evolved so our babies would be able to flourish as long as their parents nurtured them, regardless of the style their mothers and fathers followed. We wouldn't have survived as a species if every quirk of parenting had dire consequences for their child's development.

※

As children get older, their development becomes less regulated by the universal genetic program all infants are born with. Over time, a child's development is shaped by the interplay between their unique genetic profile and the environment in which they grow up, including the parenting they're exposed to. Genes determine tendencies; parents and other environmental forces influence the extent to which these tendencies are realized.

Parents make a difference, but genes impose limits on how big the difference is, especially early in life. Developmental psychologists joke that new parents believe they're in complete control of how their infant turns out, until they have a second one who turns out completely different—despite being raised the same way as their firstborn. At this point, parents realize their child-rearing only does so much in the face of genetic influences. Some parents are spectacular and some are terrible, but most are good enough.

That's why grandparents don't need to micromanage their kids' parenting. If following a schedule makes your child more comfortable, they should use one. If they discover that using a schedule drives them crazy, they shouldn't use one. By the time children are toddlers, you can tell which ones were nurtured and which ones were abused, but you can't see the difference between those whose daily lives were strictly scheduled and those whose time was less structured.

A lot of the advice in popular books for parents is meant to improve *their* lives, not their children's. There's nothing wrong with that. But to the extent that this is true, whatever approach an expert advocates should be evaluated based on how it makes parents feel, not on how their children turn out. And that's why it's pointless to argue about which generation's approach to parenting is the "right" one—with a few extreme and unusual exceptions, all of them are right as long as parents feel happy using them.

❧

A second reason to refrain from criticism is that it's a no-win situation for you. If you say something, you risk irritating your child or child-in-law and being told they want to handle it their own way. If you restrain yourself, you may be bothered by what you see or frustrated that your child's efforts aren't working. You're certain that you have an easy solution, if only they'd listen to you.

You can take the middle ground—ask your child if they'd like your advice before offering it—but you can only do that so often before it becomes annoying. And if you ask when circumstances demand an immediate action, or your child is getting agitated and impatient, you very well might get snapped at. If their baby is wailing, their toddler is kicking and screaming, or their preschooler is whining nonstop, the last thing your child wants is a question about whether it's okay to ask a question.

❧

A third reason to avoid giving advice about your child's parenting is that you may undermine their confidence at a time when they need to feel more, not less, assured about their skills in this realm. It's important that your child and their partner believe that their parenting decisions are good ones—even if they aren't perfect—

because they need to feel some control during a stressful and challenging time.

The best way to ensure your grandchild's healthy development is by making their parents feel supported and in control. This may occasionally require looking the other way when you see them doing something you wouldn't have done when you were a new parent. As long as they're good enough parents, though, it's unlikely their behavior will harm their child. Leave well enough alone. If you can't stand what you see, keep quiet and avert your eyes or leave the room. And most important: compliment your child whenever you admire how they're raising your grandchild.

❧

If you can't resist speaking up about something your child or their partner is doing, wait until later. Don't bring it up while they're doing what you disagree with. Waiting before giving your advice gives you a chance to see if it was necessary.

Suppose you and your son are chatting in the living room while the baby is napping, and the two of you hear rustling from the baby monitor. Your son gets up and walks toward the nursery. You think the rustling is normal and worry that checking on the baby will just wake them, but you hold your tongue. Your son emerges jubilant after a minute and the rustling has stopped. Instead of having told your child their judgment was bad, when in fact it wasn't, you now can say they handled things well. And if you want to help your child be a good parent, it's much more effective to praise their successes than correct their mistakes.

The closer in time between the event and your counsel, the more likely your child will take what you say as criticism rather than friendly advice—and they'll be less likely to heed it. Wait until the next day or so and say something like "You know, I've been thinking a little about what happened when you were trying to get Molly to take a bath last night and she wasn't cooperating. I have a couple of suggestions, if you'd like to hear them." Putting a little time between the difficult event and your advice about it defuses the situation and makes your child more apt to listen without getting defensive.

❧

If your child comes to you to ask for parenting advice, give it freely, but try to frame it in a way that also compliments what they've been doing.

Imagine that your daughter asks whether you think it's time to wean their baby from bottle-feeding. In your opinion, it's still too early to do this. Instead of immediately saying, "No," however, preface your advice by saying something like "Well, whatever you're doing seems to be working, because the baby is growing just fine. But it's probably okay to keep giving them a bottle for another few weeks—lots of babies wean themselves when they don't want it anymore. If they haven't by then, give your pediatrician a call and see what they say."

Or, suppose your son asks you how to respond if their three-year-old is being difficult when they're getting them dressed for preschool—every morning it's a struggle to persuade the little one to wear the clothes your son has picked out. You know from experience that the best thing to do in these situations is to select two or three acceptable options in advance and let the child choose, because allowing toddlers to make decisions supports their need to feel autonomous and grown up.

In response to your son's question, you might say, "I was watching how you handled this sort of thing so perfectly at dinner the other night, when Mikey was being difficult—you set things up as a choice between the blueberries and the strawberries, either of which you were happy to have him eat. That worked beautifully. Why not do the same thing when it comes to choosing his morning outfit?" Try to phrase your advice so your child feels even better after receiving it.

❧

The foundation of all the guidance I've offered in this part of the chapter can be summed up as follows: *When you're about to offer advice, think more about how your opinion will affect the new parents' psychological well-being than about how it will improve your grandchild's development.*

Taking care of the former will do wonders for the latter.

## You and Your Grandchild

If you want a meaningful relationship with your grandchild, you're going to have to cultivate and maintain it.

To make a good start, try to have a lot of physical contact with them during the first year, which is how newborns form attachments to others. When you hold them, make eye contact, stay attuned and responsive to their cues (like when they're signaling that they're uncomfortable, sleepy, or hungry), and speak in a soothing voice. If you do this, the chances are very good that they'll form a close bond with you.

You don't need to take care of their day-to-day needs, like feeding them, bathing them, or changing their diaper, to make this happen—so don't worry if these tasks seem too formidable or you feel out of practice. They need to be done, of course, but by themselves they don't contribute much to emotional bonding. Bonds are built by providing the baby with physical comfort. When you feed a baby, it's the holding, not the feeding, that fosters the emotional attachment.

If you live far away, visit your grandchild as frequently as you can during the first year. Phone and video calls with your child and their baby may be fun for you and the parents, but they won't do much for your grandchild so early in life. If in-person visiting isn't feasible, you'll still be able to have a close relationship as your grandchild develops, but you'll have a head start if you can spend time with them and hold them regularly during their first year.

As your grandchild gets older, you'll have to do more than cuddle them to develop a genuine friendship. When you're spending time with them, fun should be your top priority. Every interaction with a little child doesn't have to have educational value, as many of today's parents believe. I once overheard a mother in a restaurant respond to her kid's request to have dessert before finishing their string beans by saying, "Now, honey, where are green vegetables on the food pyramid?" If your child and their partner are typical of today's parents, your grandchild is already getting plenty of instruction.

If you have an inquisitive grandchild who asks about nature, wants to tell you about a book they read in school, or likes talking about movies they've seen, by all means, talk about those topics with them. But if your six-year-old wants to play Monopoly, enjoy the game without using the financial transactions as a math class. In the long run, your grandchild will remember the times you spent laughing together much more than your lessons.

❧

When you phone your child's family to check in, once your grandchild can talk, ask to speak to them, too. Initially, your conversations may feel a bit forced, but as your grandchild becomes more accustomed to hearing from you, they'll start to open up, and you'll be surprised at how talkative they can be. Get in the habit of calling every so often just to speak with your grandchild, or calling your grandchild's cell phone, once they have their own. This will reinforce the idea that they have a special relationship with you that doesn't need to always involve their parents. As they get older, they'll start to see you as another person they can turn to for support and friendship. Lots of grandparents text, email, and share social media with their grandchildren. You'll learn a lot about technology from them—as long as you're patient with each other.

Develop a special routine or find a special outing that you and your grandchild enjoy doing alone together that's something you'll be able to keep doing even as they get older. A friend of mine has to travel a fair distance to visit her grandson, but once he was old enough to appreciate eating in a nice restaurant, they developed an annual tradition of dressing up and going to a favorite restaurant— just the two of them—for a fancy lunch. They began doing this when her grandson was just entering elementary school, and they have done it ever since—and he's now in college. It doesn't have to be dining out, but find an activity to enjoy privately with your grandchild regularly, and make it something the two of you look forward to and plan together.

Take an interest in your grandchild's interests. It's fine to ask how school is going, but most children quickly tire of this question because so many people ask it (and many parents ask it every evening). If you do ask about school, make your questions specific—ask about a particular class, a favorite teacher, a special classmate, or a project they're working on. But try to find something else to talk about, too—something your grandchild is enthusiastic about. True, many kids are enthusiastic about school, but even those who love it usually have other interests. If your grandchild is a baseball nut, learn enough about the sport to enjoy watching and discussing it with them. If they have a collection of some sort, ask to see any new additions when you visit. If they like music, ask them what they've been listening to lately and have them play a sample for you.

And don't forget to share *your* interests with your grandchild. You may well have hobbies or activities or favorites they would enjoy hearing about. Tell your grandchild about things you've read recently, trips you've taken (and if you have them, share some photos or videos), TV shows you've enjoyed, or things you've been thinking or wondering about. Don't do this with an educational goal in mind—just talk about things the way you would with a friend. Ask for their opinions—children like to feel that grown-ups value their views. Parents are often too busy to break out of the parental role and do this. As a grandparent without the same responsibilities as a parent, you'll have a lot of time for fun conversations with your grandchild.

Spend some time with your grandchild in situations that don't include their parents—sometimes by yourselves, sometimes with your partner, and, if you have more than one grandchild, with one or more of their siblings or cousins. If you limit socializing with them to family gatherings, they won't get to know you very well as a *person*, beyond knowing you as a grandparent. They may have questions they're dying to ask you but are shy about asking in front of everyone else. And they may have things to tell you that their parents already know, or that they don't want to talk about when their parents are around. Many children love having an adult other than their parents as a confidant, and you may be the perfect person for that, especially if the two of you have been close for a long time.

Share stories about your family's history. You're an important repository of information about your family, and you should share it with your grandchild while you can. If your grandchild is in elementary school, a fun project to share is creating a family tree with the names, birth places, and birth dates of as many relatives as you can think of. If you kept a diary as a child and feel comfortable sharing parts of it, your grandchild will find it fascinating.

Most children especially like hearing about their parents' and their grandparents' childhood and adolescent years, both because they reveal what life was like long ago (or what seems long ago to a child) and because they find it intriguing to imagine their parents and grandparents as kids. The stories shouldn't be embarrassing, but they can be amusing or reveal special talents or accomplishments of yours or their parents that they weren't aware of—that you were into scouting, their mother won a statewide poetry contest, or their father used to entertain the family with magic tricks at holiday get-togethers.

If recent immigration is part of your family's history, your grandchild would probably love to hear about how your family first emigrated, where they settled, what they did to survive when they arrived, and what life was like for them before they emigrated. Learning about the family's heritage is especially important when your grandchild is an adolescent and beginning to put together their own sense of identity. You can help ensure that important aspects of your culture become part of how they think about themselves.

❧

Your grandchild may still be too young for you to think of as a friend, but they may become one as they get older. Grandchildren also can be an important source of assistance and support when their grandparents are elderly. Once your grandchild is a teenager, they can be extremely helpful, especially with physical projects that require the strength or agility of youth. I've known grandchildren who helped their grandparents repair a rickety deck, did housekeeping while a grandparent was recovering from a fall, or drove their grandparents around when they needed to run errands. You may not need your grandchild's assistance now, and they may still be too young to provide it, but developing and maintaining a strong relationship with them when they're young will make it that much easier to depend on them when you need help down the road. And that experience will be just as important for them as it is for you.

It's understandable and correct that society emphasizes parents' influence on their children's well-being. But grandparents who are actively engaged in their grandchild's life also contribute in important ways to their grandchild's development, probably more than they realize.

And it works both ways. When I began writing this chapter, our grandson, Henry, was around a year old, and when I could tell that he and I were already developing a close bond—when he started to get excited when I walked into the room or when we invented our own version of hide-and-seek that would make him shriek with laughter—the feeling was indescribable, an emotional high like nothing I've ever felt before.

## CHAPTER NINE

# Summing Up and Looking Ahead

Summing Up
Looking Ahead

## Summing Up

If there's one crucial takeaway from this book, it's that parenting an adult child is very different today than it was a generation ago. This has left many parents perplexed about their relationship with their child.

Several factors have contributed to this situation. First, because the passage from adolescence into adulthood now is so prolonged, many challenges parents faced when their children were in their late teens and early twenties have been pushed into the mid-twenties, late twenties, or beyond. This shift has created new dynamics that alter the nature of the discussions parents might have with their adult children. Someone who would have openly expressed concerns about their child's choice of a romantic partner when their child was twenty-three may be hesitant to do so now that their child is thirty-five. A parent whose twenty-two-year-old asked for $100 would feel entitled to ask what the money is for and say whether this is a wise expenditure. If the child were thirty-three at the time of the request, a parent might wonder if asking the question or expressing an opinion was appropriate.

Second, the changed timetable of young adulthood has made it difficult for parents to tell whether their child is floundering, flourishing, or something in between. A generation ago, a parent might have worried about a child who was in their early thirties and still single. Today, being unattached at that age is very common and no cause for concern. In the past, people graduated from college when they were twenty-two and started a career almost immediately. Today, many people don't graduate until they're twenty-four or twenty-five, and might not settle into a career until they're thirty. My parents would have worried about my career if I hadn't made much progress by the time I turned thirty. By today's standards, though, not establishing a career by that age is par for the course. In other words, what may have looked like floundering in love or work a generation ago is no longer floundering today—but many parents don't realize this.

Third, because today's parents probably hadn't thought much about what it means to have an adult child, they approached this phase of their family's life believing that parenting would be a breeze compared to raising an adolescent. Many soon discover that their relationship with their adult child brings its own challenges. They're often taken by surprise and unsure what to do when they are. Whenever a child enters a new stage of development, parents have to figure out whether and how they should change their approach to their child. This uncertainty often fuels parents' anxiety over whether they're doing too much or too little. They may even be too nervous to ask their child this very question! Many parents discover they're riding an emotional roller coaster during a time in their child's life that they had expected would be stress-free.

Fourth, because young people have postponed many of the traditional transitions into adulthood—completing college, settling down with a romantic partner, achieving financial independence, and becoming a parent—their social status is unclear to their parents and themselves. On the one hand, they feel emotionally mature, and in all likelihood they are. On the other hand, their lives still retain some of the trappings of adolescence. They're dating rather than married, in school rather than employed, financially dependent on their parents rather than self-sufficient. This leaves them just as uncertain as their parents about what constitutes an appropriate relationship between them. Ambiguity in a relationship between two people can make their interactions awkward.

Finally, as if all this wasn't challenging enough, society has changed in many ways that make becoming an independent adult harder, mainly because of transformations in the labor force and the housing market, both of which require staying in school longer and waiting longer to establish one's own household. This, in turn, has created strain that's been exacerbated by other societal events, such as the Great Recession and the COVID-19 pandemic.

You may think that today's twenty- and thirtysomethings have been coddled, but it's demonstrably tougher to be a young adult now than it was thirty years ago, when you were about their age. It's clear that this challenge has taken its toll on the mental health of young people, which by many measures has worsened considerably over the past two decades—and which was declining well before COVID-19 struck. Coping with an adult child who's anxious, depressed, addicted, or even suicidal is very difficult, and more parents than ever before have been placed in this agonizing position.

Together, these changes have created conflicts over autonomy that are at the heart of most tensions between parents and their adult children. Both generations are unsure about what's reasonable to expect from each other, and many parents find that they walk on eggshells, fearing being labeled as intrusive (if they try to stay as involved in their child's life as they had been before) or uncaring (if they've pulled back). At times it feels like you can't win. Adult children have their own balancing act to contend with, too, working through conflicts over their own sense of autonomy and identity as adults while being forced by society to remain dependent on their parents for longer than they'd like.

❧

Throughout this book, I've advised approaches that parents with adult children can take in many realms to maintain a strong bond during this challenging time. Here's a quick summary of my main points:

First, *don't use the timeline you followed as a young adult to judge your child's progress.* Stop saying, or even thinking, "When I was your age." It's an inappropriate and unhelpful way to think about how your kid is doing.

Second, *recognize and support your child's need to establish autonomy from you,* which will intensify as they approach their thirties. Don't get upset when they choose not to follow your advice or tell you, in so many words, to mind your own business. Remember, it's not about you. It's about your child's need to show you, themselves, and the world that they're mature and competent enough to handle adulthood without relying on their parents.

Third, *examine whether your expectations for this relationship are reasonable.* Don't force yourself to have low expectations because you would rather be pleasantly surprised than disappointed. Low expectations have a way of bringing out the worst in others. But don't expect things to be problem-free, either.

Fourth, *take time to analyze your own emotions when you feel hurt by your kid*. All parents have unpleasant feelings about their kids from time to time—they feel neglected, unappreciated, disrespected, or annoyed. This is perfectly normal, and nothing to be ashamed of. But sometimes your bad feelings are due to your interpretation of your child's behavior and not really about what your child has or hasn't done.

Fifth, *try not to ruminate*, either alone or in conversation with a friend, about experiences with your child that have hurt or disappointed you. Once you've had a chance to step back and figure out what's bothering you, let your child know what you're feeling. And don't be afraid to seek counseling if you get into a rut you can't climb out of.

Sixth, *learn how to resolve disputes with your child constructively*. I've given specific advice on this topic throughout the book and illustrated good and bad ways to do this with anecdotes about other families. When you can, engage in "collaborative problem-solving," an effective way of finding out what each of you thinks is contributing to the disagreement and what steps you can take to remedy it. When two people put their heads together to jointly arrive at the solution to a problem, it's much more likely to be effective than if one does it alone.

Finally, when trying to decide whether to voice your opinion or bite your tongue, use this general principle: *Speak up when you must, but unless your child specifically asks for your opinion, keep it to yourself.* The exceptions to this guidance are situations in which your kid, their partner, or their child are potentially exposed to grave and irreparable harm.

If you can follow these suggestions often, you'll be laying a strong foundation for the future of your relationship with your adult child. And that foundation may prove essential in the long term. While working on this book, I heard from many parents who are facing a challenging time with a child who's in their forties or fifties. As I've said, parenting never ends.

## Looking Ahead

Although your relationship with your adult child will keep evolving after they reach their forties, it will likely become more stable in some ways. Your child has made the transition from a period that's typically filled with major life changes—graduating, starting a career, settling down with a partner, establishing their own household, achieving financial independence, starting a family—to one that's usually more predictable and static. For most people, the forties is a time of consolidation and incremental change, both psychologically and socially. If things have gone well, people tend to find their footing during this decade—their careers progress, their marriages evolve, their children grow into adolescence, but core personality traits tend to stabilize.

Because the major transitions that defined your child's twenties and thirties have been completed, many of the challenges they prompted for you as a parent probably have been settled. Some parents may still harbor concerns that their child's career has stalled, their romantic life is unsettled, their finances are shaky, or their parenting is worrisome, but these are exceptions to the rule. Moreover, if there are unresolved issues in any of these domains, there's probably little you can do to help other than providing emotional support and a sympathetic ear.

Psychologically, your child has probably worked through any issues having to do with their autonomy from you. Once they've established themselves as independent and capable, they don't need to assert themselves to demonstrate their competence to you. They no longer have to disagree with or dismiss your views just for the sake of it. You'll find that this has a calming effect on your relationship.

One very pleasant consequence of this is that your opinions generally will become more valued and your advice more likely to be accepted, because your child is no longer threatened by your authority. You'll find far less need to bite your tongue. This doesn't give you license to dispense unsolicited advice about every decision your middle-aged child faces, but it should make you feel easier about giving it when it's necessary. And you'll find that your child, now more secure and confident than before, is more willing to seek your wisdom on issues they're undecided about.

Any challenges that arise during this time will probably have more to do with what's taking place in *your* life, not your child's. As you move toward and through your seventies, you'll likely go through major transitions of your own—among them, retirement, relocation, and dealing with the expected changes in mental and physical abilities that normally come with aging. For some people, the seventies is a time when health concerns, both minor and serious, may arise. There's a reason that, when COVID-19 vaccines first became available, people over sixty-five were among the first groups to receive them. Even healthy people at this age are more vulnerable to disease, illness, and injury than they were a decade earlier.

❧

Changes in your child's life circumstances during their twenties and thirties created new issues in your relationship with them. Now changes in your life circumstances will do something similar.

As your child moves toward their forties and you toward your seventies, your relationship will go through a bit of a role reversal as you find yourself increasingly more dependent on them and they less so on you.

This is both gratifying and disconcerting. It's gratifying because someone who was once your helpless infant, who relied on you or your partner for everything, has grown into somebody you can turn to for advice and assistance—in part because of how you raised them. But it's also disconcerting, because sometimes it's all too apparent that when the two of you are alone together, you may no longer be the smartest or most capable person in the room, a position you've occupied for four decades.

This role reversal will take some getting used to, but be grateful you have someone you can lean on. Maybe even literally.

Fortunately, this change in your relationship won't all happen at once—it will be incremental and occur at different rates in different domains, depending on your needs and your child's availability and capability. Every so often you may need your child's physical help if your strength, agility, or balance is wavering. You may occasionally ask for some advice about managing your investments or downloading an app that creates, stores, and automatically completes your online passwords (something you should probably have). Depending on how technologically savvy you are, you might need some help selecting and setting up a new electronic device, unfreezing a computer or smartphone, or choosing among different internet plans.

None of this is surprising, nor should it be concerning. Someone who's three decades younger than you is likely to be in better shape, more skillful with numbers and information (especially in the fast-changing digital world), and more knowledgeable about the latest technological innovations.

You've been able to compensate for the natural decline in some raw abilities that comes with age by drawing on wisdom and experience. But no amount of either will help you balance on a ladder while cleaning out the gutters, carry a fifty-pound carton of books up to the attic, dig a hole to plant a new shrub, set up a new smartphone, or configure a wireless sound system so that it works with your music streaming service. Asking your child for help isn't a problem. Feeling bad about doing so is.

This role reversal may evoke three uncomfortable emotions that are important to examine and reframe: anxiety, embarrassment, and guilt.

*Anxiety.* The change in your relative dependency on each other is a reminder that you're getting older, which few of us relish. But getting older isn't the same as becoming infirm, and just because you're a couple of steps slower or can't lift quite as much as you could ten years ago, or need stronger reading glasses, hearing aids to watch a movie without turning on subtitles, or a walking stick when you go for hikes doesn't mean this is the beginning of the end. After all, you're still staying up on the news, enjoying your favorite programs, and staying active—you just need a little extra time or equipment to do so. And if you're in good health, you're probably going to be around for many more years.

Don't let an implicit comparison with your child cause you to age less gracefully.

The fact that they may be at the peak of their health is irrelevant to the state of yours. Comparing your physical abilities to those of a thirty-year-old makes as much sense as them comparing their lifetime accomplishments to those of someone your age. Aging has its liabilities, but it also has its benefits. If you start to feel older because of something your child now does better than you, make sure to look at both sides of the ledger. You may not be as fast on the tennis court as your child, but you may be much better at driving a golf ball off the tee, which is more about technique than brute force. If you're concerned about your physical fitness, instead of comparing yourself unfavorably to your child, exercise more.

Your anxiety about growing older may also be affected by your awareness that your child is intellectually sharper than you. There is a normal, age-related decline in certain aspects of intellectual functioning, mainly memory, that begins in the mid- to late forties. For some people the changes are imperceptible, but for others they may have modest effects on learning and recalling new information. It's possible you'll become a little more forgetful and a little slower at performing new tasks. Comparing yourself with your child when you're playing a word or trivia game—when "tip of the tongue" memory lapses can be common—may make you a little self-conscious. These changes are to be expected, though, and don't signal any sort of dementia. Moreover, if they don't have any impact on your day-to-day life, don't worry about them. A healthy diet, socializing, and physical exercise are good for cognitive functioning, too, as is learning new things. If you feel like you've lost a bit of intellectual sparkle, take a course in something you've always been interested in, either online or in person, learn to play a new musical instrument, or take up a new hobby. Novelty and challenge keep a brain healthy longer.

*Embarrassment.* A second concern is that this role reversal will change your child's view of you in a way that somehow diminishes your stature in their eyes. Frankly, I doubt your child bases their evaluation of you on whether you need their assistance with some task or you've gotten slower at guessing the answers on *Jeopardy!* Their feelings and opinions about you have been shaped by the long history of your relationship—hopefully a positive one filled with love and admiration. It won't be shaken by asking them for help or advice.

It's likely your self-perceptions are more affected by these changes in your abilities than your child's view of you is. In fact, your child may not even notice some of the very changes that bother you or make you self-conscious. I can recall meeting my son and daughter-in-law at a restaurant for dinner after not having seen each other for three months during which I began wearing hearing aids. My vanity had gotten the better of me, and I was nervous about looking like an old man. After we had been at the table for a while and neither of them had said anything about the new devices, I assumed they were just being polite. Finally, I said, "You haven't said anything about my hearing aids." In fact, they hadn't even noticed them.

Don't let pride stop you from asking your child for help if they can do something you need done. And just because you need assistance with one thing doesn't mean you need help with everything. Just take it one request at a time. Don't keep a running mental tally of the things you've asked them to do for you, which will magnify your embarrassment about becoming slightly more dependent on them. You're probably not keeping track of all the ways in which you continue to assist your child, so your balance sheet is likely to be skewed. The role reversal is gradual, and an increase in the ways you depend on your child doesn't mean they won't still call on you when they need to.

Asking a child for financial assistance is hard for many parents to do, because asking a son or daughter to help with a task that requires strength or specialized knowledge is predictable, whereas asking for money usually is unanticipated. It was once commonplace for children to help their parents financially, though, and it was no more unusual in the past than parents helping their children is today. People of all ages have occasional financial emergencies, and there's nothing to be embarrassed about if you're in the midst of one. Your child may not have the resources necessary to help you out, but there is no harm in asking, and I doubt they'll think any less of you if you do.

*Guilt.* Some parents are worried that asking their child for assistance or advice will be burdensome, and they may hesitate to ask because they feel guilty. Your child, whom you've helped for the past several decades, won't feel burdened by an occasional request for help or advice. When you provided help as a parent, I suspect you got pleasure out of doing so. Why on earth would your child not feel the same way about assisting you? It's what people in healthy families do for each other happily and readily.

If you're asking for something especially onerous, precede it with some sort of explanation, but don't start with an apology. You don't need to justify asking someone with whom you've had a forty- or fifty-year relationship to do you a favor, even a big one.

❦

The conflicts over autonomy you and your child had when they were younger will dissipate once you both come to a new understanding about your relationship. You'll start seeing them in a different light and appreciate how mature they are. You may seek their opinion more often about decisions you're contemplating. At the same time, they'll gain a new perspective on you as they come to better understand the demands and responsibilities of adulthood and see how much you have in common. They now see what it's like to have a family depend on you for financial and emotional support. They know what it feels like to be a boss or to be bossed by someone else. If they're a parent, they've discovered both the pleasures and difficulties inherent in raising a child, and they may have newfound respect and appreciation for how you raised them.

As you both become more accustomed to this new phase of

your relationship, you'll find it's more equitable than it was just a few years before. You no longer need to act as if you're more knowledgeable, confident, or infallible than you know you are. In many ways, this is liberating. You'll feel more comfortable speaking openly about your feelings, about the good and bad decisions you've made over the course of your life, and about your worries and concerns.

In exchange for being open, there's a good possibility the two of you will develop a deeper friendship than you've ever had with them before. Few people have known you for as long or as intimately as your child has, and few relationships have been as close. Now that you've let go of some of the prerogatives of parenthood, you'll likely find your child to be a source of emotional support, a good listener, a good teacher who knows more than you do about many things, and a good companion.

It took a long time and great effort to reach this point in your relationship. Now it's time to revel in it.

# Acknowledgments

I could not have written this book without the encouragement, love, and support of my wife, co-parent, and co-grandparent, Wendy, who not only read and edited several versions of the manuscript, but whose great wisdom about parenting and grandparenting helped me clarify and improve my own thinking about being the parent of adult children. She's been a great teacher and a fabulous role model.

Several colleagues and friends read and commented on earlier drafts of this book, and their suggestions improved it a great deal. I'm indebted to C. Jama Adams, Jay Belsky, Angela Duckworth, David Harmon, Todd Mann, Lawrence Peltz, Joseph Ryan, Susan Stockdale, Barrie Trimmingham, Marsha Weinraub, Felecia Weiss, and Jeff Weiss.

Thanks to AARP for coming up with the idea for this book, and special thanks to Jodi Lipson at AARP for her editorial wisdom. I also am grateful to the entire team at Simon & Schuster, including Tzipora Baitch, Phil Metcalf, Zoe Kaplan, and Alexis Minieri.

Finally, I thank my agent, Jim Levine, and my editor, Eamon Dolan, for suggesting I take this project on, for their sage advice on how to structure and shape the book, and for their many excellent editorial suggestions.

# Notes

Chapter One: Your Evolving Role as a Parent

6  *substantial changes take place in the brain's anatomy and activity*: "White Paper on the Science of Late Adolescence: A Guide for Judges, Attorneys and Policy Makers," Center for Law, Brain & Behavior, Massachusetts General Hospital, October 2022, https://clbb.mgh.harvard.edu/white-paper-on-the-science-of-late-adolescence.

8  *Today's jobs require more years of schooling than they did a generation ago*: Anna Brown, "Key Findings About the American Workforce and the Changing Job Market," Pew Research Center, October 2016, https://www.pewresearch.org/fact-tank/2016/10/06/key-findings-about-the-american-workforce-and-the-changing-job-market/.

8  *now takes the average U.S. college student five years or more*: Data come from the National Center for Education Statistics, U.S. Department of Education, 2019.

8  *statistics published by the Census Bureau and other government agencies*: Data on age at college graduation come from the National Center for Education Statistics; data on age at marriage and birth of first child come from the U.S. Census Bureau.

26  *the average price of a home rose five times faster than the average salary*: Gregory Schmidt, "Wages Can't Keep Up with Housing Prices," *New York Times*, May 8, 2022.

## Chapter Two: Growing Together

30    *this sort of permanent estrangement is very rare*: Lucy Blake, "Parents and Children Who Are Estranged in Adulthood: A Review and Discussion of the Literature," *Journal of Family Theory Review* 9, no. 4 (2017): 521–36.

36    *co-rumination is sometimes worse for your well-being than ruminating alone*: Leonardo Carlucci et al., "Co-Rumination, Anxiety, and Maladaptive Cognitive Schemas: When Friendship Can Hurt," *Psychology Research and Behavior Management* 1, no. 1 (2018): 133–44.

## Chapter Three: Mental Health

50    *adolescents and young adults are most vulnerable to mental health problems*: R. C. Kessler et al., "Lifetime Prevalence and Age-of-Onset Distributions of DSM-IV Disorders in the National Comorbidity Survey Replication," *Archives of General Psychiatry* 62, no. 6 (2005): 593–602; National Research Council, *Investing in the Health and Well-Being of Young Adults* (Washington, DC: National Academies Press, 2015).

50    *The prevalence of mental health problems among young people has risen dramatically*: "Data and Statistics on Children's Mental Health," Centers for Disease Control and Prevention, https://www.cdc.gov/childrensmentalhealth/data.html. Retrieved September 30, 2022.

50    *major depressive episodes among adults in other age groups were unchanged*: Jean Twenge et al., "Age, Period, and Cohort Trends in Mood Disorder Indicators and Suicide Related Outcomes in a Nationally Representative Dataset, 2005–2017," *Journal of Abnormal Psychology* 128, no. 3 (2019): 185–99.

50    *Suicidal thinking rose dramatically among young adults*: Twenge et al., "Age, Period, and Cohort Trends."

50    *staggering increase in mental health problems*: Nirmita Panchal et al., "The Implications of COVID-19 for Mental Health and Substance Use," Kaiser Family Foundation, February 10, 2021, https://www.kff.org/coronavirus-covid-19/issue-brief/the-implications-of-covid-19-for-mental-health-and-substance-use/.

51    *an especially severe toll on the psychological health of young adults*: Nimita Panchal, "Recent Trends in Mental Health and Substance Use Concerns Among Adolescents," Kaiser Family Foundation, June 28, 2022, https://www.kff.org/coronavirus-covid-19/issue-brief/recent-trends-in-mental-health-and-substance-use-concerns-among-adolescents/.

## Chapter Four: Education

83    *The vast majority of the world's richest people graduated from college*: Deniz Çam, "Doctorate, Degree, or Dropout: How Much Education It Takes to Become a Billionaire," *Forbes*, October 18, 2017, https://www.forbes.com/sites/denizcam/2017/10/18/doctorate-degree-or-dropout-how-much-education-it-takes-to-become-a-billionaire.

84    *about 40 percent of college freshmen never end up graduating*: "College Dropout Rates," ThinkImpact, (2021), https://www.thinkimpact.com/college-dropout-rates/.

88    *"lawn mower parents"*: Nicole Pelletiere, "Move Aside Helicopter Moms, Lawnmower Parents Are on the Rise," GMA, September 18, 2018, www.goodmorningamerica.com/family/story/move-helicopter-moms-lawnmower-parents-rise-57805055.

88    *Forty percent of college students who drop out do so for financial reasons*: "New Research Answers Question Every College Wants to Know: Why Do Students Leave and How Do We Get Them Back?," University Professional and Continuing Education Association, December 1, 2021, https://upcea.edu/new-research-answers-question-every-college-wants-to-know-why-do-students-leave-and-how-do-we-get-them-back/.

92    *About half of entering college students need at least one remedial class*: Laura Jiminez, "The Cost of Catching Up," Center for American Progress, September 28, 2016, https://www.americanprogress.org/article/remedial-education/.

92    *students who need such classes are more likely to drop out than their peers*: Michael Nietzel, "Remedial Education: Escaping Higher

Education's Hotel California," *Forbes*, October 22, 2018, https://www.forbes.com/sites/michaeltnietzel/2018/10/22/remedial-education-escaping-higher-educations-hotel-california.

## Chapter Five: Finances

122    *one frequently recommended guideline*: "The 40-70 Rule: Communicating Touchy Topics," Home Instead, October 1, 2020, www.homeinstead.com/care-resources/care-planning/communicating-touchy-topics/.

## Chapter Six: Romance and Marriage

136    *Only about one-fourth of today's married people met their spouse in college*: Kelsey Campbell-Dollaghan, "Facebook Data Shows How Many People Graduate College with True Love," Gizmodo, October 7, 2013, https://gizmodo.com/facebook-data-shows-how-many-people-graduate-college-wi-1442070364.

136    *the average age at which people met their future spouse*: Serina Sandhu, "British People Meet Lifelong Partner at 27, Study Reveals," *Independent*, January 19, 2016, https://www.independent.co.uk/news/uk/home-news/british-people-meet-lifelong-partner-at-27-study-reveals-a6820431.html.

147    *females are more social*: Marco Del Giudice, "Gender Differences in Personality and Social Behavior," in *International Encyclopedia of the Social & Behavioral Sciences,* 2nd ed., vol. 9, ed. James D. Wright (Amsterdam: Elsevier Science, 2015), 750–56.

154    *All couples argue*: Katherine McGonagle et al., "The Frequency and Determinants of Marital Disagreements in a Community Sample," *Journal of Social and Personal Relationships* 9, no. 4 (1992): 507–24. Although this classic study is thirty years old, more recent surveys have reached similar conclusions. See Taylor Orth, "How and Why Do American Couples Argue?," YouGovAmerica, June 1, 2022, https://today.yougov.com/topics/society/articles-reports/2022/06/01/how-and-why-do-american-couples-argue.

155    *More than a quarter of all homicides*: Aaron Kivisto and Megan Porter, "Firearm Use Increases Risk of Multiple Victims in Domestic Homicides," *Journal of the American Academy of Psychiatry and the Law* 48, no. 1 (2020): 26–34.

156    *stay married for at least twenty years*: Wendy Wang, "The Link Between a College Education and a Lasting Marriage," Pew Research Center, December 4, 2015, https://www.pewresearch.org/fact-tank/2015/12/04/education-and-marriage/.

156    *divorce became even less common than it was before*: Wendy D. Manning and Krista K. Westrick-Payne, "Marriage and Divorce During the COVID-19 Pandemic: A Case Study of Five States," *Socius: Sociological Research for a Dynamic World* 7 (2021): 1–3.

157    *people's mental health following a divorce*: Anna Kołodziej-Zaleska and Hanna Przybyła-Basista, "Psychological Well-Being of Individuals After Divorce: The Role of Social Support," *Current Issues in Personality Psychology* 4, no. 4 (2016): 206–16.

158    *if their parents are fighting all the time*: E. Mark Cummings and Patrick T. Davies, *Children and Marital Conflict: The Impact of Family Dispute and Resolution* (New York: Guilford Press, 1994).

159    *difficulties faced by the divorcees*: Jennifer Lansford, "Parental Divorce and Children's Adjustment," *Perspectives on Psychological Science* 4, no. 2 (2009): 140–52.

## Chapter Seven: Flourishing or Floundering?

162    *a model of flourishing*: Margaret Kern et al., "The EPOCH Measure of Adolescent Well-Being," *Psychological Assessment* 28, no. 5 (2016): 586–97. This measure is not designed for use beyond high school, but a similar perspective, called PERMA, which applies to young adults, can be found at https://positivepsychology.com/perma-model/. Retrieved September 30, 2022.

165    *Some students take considerably longer*: Data come from the National Center for Education Statistics, U.S. Department of Education, 2019.

178    *More than a quarter of American undergraduates*: Data come from

the National Center for Education Statistics, U.S. Department of Education, 2021.

181 *the average American woman got married*: Data come from the Current Population Survey, U.S. Census Bureau, which provides this information annually.

181 *according to recent estimates*: Richard Reeves and Christopher Pulliam, "Middle Class Marriage Is Declining, and Likely Deepening Inequality," Brookings Institution, March 11, 2020, https://www.brookings.edu/research/middle-class-marriage-is-declining-and-likely-deepening-inequality/.

182 *nonmarried people between the ages of twenty-five and thirty-four who are living with a partner*: Benjamin Gurrentz, "Living with an Unmarried Partner Now Common for Young Adults," U.S. Census Bureau, November 15, 2018, https://www.census.gov/library/stories/2018/11/cohabitation-is-up-marriage-is-down-for-young-adults.html; Juliana Horowitz et al., "Marriage and Cohabitation in the U.S.," Pew Research Center, November 6, 2019, https://www.pewresearch.org/social-trends/2019/11/06/marriage-and-cohabitation-in-the-u-s/.

182 *say they hope to get hitched one day*: Bella De Paulo, "How Many Americans Want to Be Single?" *Psychology Today*, September 20, 2017, https://www.psychologytoday.com/us/blog/living-single/201709/how-many-americans-want-be-single-results-5-studies.

182 *cohabitation has become an enduring way of life*: W. Bradford Wilcox and Wendy Wang, "The Marriage Divide: How and Why Working-Class Families Are More Fragile Today," Research Brief for Opportunity America–AEI–Brookings Working Class Group, September 2017, https://www.aei.org/wp-content/uploads/2017/09/The-Marriage-Divide.pdf?x91208.

182 *preceded by some period of cohabitation*: Wendy D. Manning and Lisa Carlson, "Trends in Cohabitation Prior to Marriage," National Center for Family & Marriage Research, Bowling Green State University, April 13, 2021, https://www.bgsu.edu/ncfmr

/resources/data/family-profiles/manning-carlson-trends-co-habitation-marriage-fp-21-04.html.

183 *have never been married*: American Community Survey, "Never Married on the Rise," U.S. Census Bureau (2020), https://www.census.gov/content/dam/Census/library/visualizations/2021/comm/unmarried-americans.pdf.

183 *one-third of all unmarried people in their late thirties*: Data on age at first marriage come from the U.S. Census Bureau.

183 *IVF is successful half the time*: Data come from the Society for Assisted Reproductive Technology, https://www.today.com/parents/pregnancy/ivf-success-rate-rcna38775. Retrieved September 30, 2022.

184 *they just don't want to be parents*: Anna Brown, "Growing Share of Childless Adults in U.S. Don't Expect to Ever Have Children," Pew Research Center, November 19, 2021, https://www.pewresearch.org/fact-tank/2021/11/19/growing-share-of-childless-adults-in-u-s-dont-expect-to-ever-have-children/.

185 *being in love was the main reason*: Juliana Horowitz et al., "Why People Get Married or Move In with a Partner," Pew Research Center, November 6, 2019, https://www.pewresearch.org/social-trends/2019/11/06/why-people-get-married-or-move-in-with-a-partner/.

186 *More young adults now live with their parents*: The discussion on young adults moving back home draws on data from Richard Fry et al., "A Majority of Young Adults in the U.S. Live with Their Parents for the First Time Since the Great Depression," Pew Research Center, September 4, 2020, https://www.pewresearch.org/fact-tank/2020/09/04/a-majority-of-young-adults-in-the-u-s-live-with-their-parents-for-the-first-time-since-the-great-depression/.

193 *they and their parents get along fine*: Bella De Paulo, "Why Are So Many Young Adults Living with Their Parents?" *Psychology Today*, May 26, 2016, https://www.psychologytoday.com/us/blog/living-single/201605/why-are-so-many-young-adults-living-their-parents.

# NOTES

## Chapter Eight: Grandparenthood

196 *A close connection with a grandchild*: Donald C. Reitzes and Elizabeth J. Mutran, "Grandparent Identity, Intergenerational Family Identity, and Well-Being," *Journals of Gerontology: Series B* 59, no. 4 (2004): S213–S219.

198 *short-term postpartum depression*: "Baby Blues," American Pregnancy Association, https://americanpregnancy.org/healthy-pregnancy/first-year-of-life/baby-blues/. Retrieved September 30, 2022.

## Chapter Nine: Summing Up and Looking Ahead

224 *begins in the mid- to late forties*: K. Warner Schaie, "The Course of Adult Intellectual Development," *American Psychologist* 49, no. 4 (1994): 304–13.

# Index

# INDEX